EMOTIONAL
SELF
MASTERY

*The Best Book on Regaining Personal Power,
Self-Confidence, and Peace*

By Cheryl C Jones

*"I'll teach you how to clean up your stinkin'
thinkin' and negative self-talk, so, you can master
not only your emotions but your life."*

Published by
Can Do Press
1730 Cactus Bluff
San Antonio, TX 78258
210-545-2378

Emotional Self Mastery: The best book on regaining personal power, Confidence, and peace / Cheryl C. Jones

ISBN 978-1-7326478-0-0

ISBN eBook 978-1-7326478-1-7

BISAC: Self Help | Personal Growth | Self Esteem

Dedication

To those who have felt stuck, frustrated or emotionally imprisoned by negativity and longed for a solution.

Acknowledgements

I wish to thank those whose encouragement and support helped bring this book into being. Many thanks to:

Tami Gulland, my business coach and dear friend, for helping me clear the hidden limiting beliefs that slowed the process of getting this book completed and for keeping me on track as my accountability partner.

Kathi Holzschuher, my one-of-a-kind BFF, for her support as a cheerleader for me and this project, and for her help in editing the manuscript.

My dear sweet husband, Marvin Jones who knew there was a book inside me just teeming to get out. Thank you for your patience and encouragement as I took this journey through the many changes and drafts. I appreciate your support and your love each and every day. I love our wonderful life together.

Christopher Jones and Jo Jones, our sons, who have taught me how to successfully be in a relationship with them on an in-the-moment basis and to meet them where they are without judgment.

Beverly B. Crane, PhD, my mom, for her continuous belief in me and her willingness to share her expertise and psychological insights.

Jan Waddy, for her willingness to be an advance reader of this manuscript, providing valuable feedback, and a lifetime of friendship.

Blake Griffin for graciously illustrating how messages are morphed into beliefs.

Joe Vitale, author of two of my favorite books, *The Attractor Factor: 5 Steps to Creating Wealth (Or Anything Else) from the Inside Out* and *Anything Is Possible*, for his inspiration and reminder that *anything* truly IS possible—even completing this book.

Kent Cummins and other fellow members of the Austin Chapter of the National Speakers Association's Writers SIG (Special Interest Group) for their encouragement to keep writing even when I was struggling to get words on the page.

Disclaimer

The purpose of this book is to help you develop greater self-awareness and control over your undesired thoughts and emotional responses to events, people, and situations, so that you easily build the life you wish to live and readily reach your goals. This book is intended to be a resource that encourages, informs, and inspires. It is in no way meant to replace the advice of qualified medical or other health care providers.

The stories contained within are based on true accounts and personal experiences. In many cases, the names of those involved have been changed to ensure privacy.

While the publisher, designers, editors, and author have done their best to prepare this edition, they make no warranties or representations with respect to the accuracy or completeness of the contents and disclaim any implied warranties of results when applying strategies, tools, or techniques contained within. Neither the publisher, designers, editors, nor the author shall be liable for any injury, personal or otherwise, as a result of applying the techniques within. The reader assumes full responsibility for his or her own physical safety and mental well-being.

Table Of Contents

Section One
Emotional Self-Mastery Leads to Happiness

Section Two
Changing the Head Games

Section Three
Shifting the Energy

Foreword By Dr. Joe Vitale

One morning early in 2018, I told a small group of professional speakers about my career as an author. They knew about my movie appearance in The Secret. They had a basic knowledge of my line of books, with *The Attractor Factor* and *Zero Limits* touching many.

But they didn't know the whole story. I mentioned that one of my early books was a sixteen-page pamphlet called *Turbocharge Your Writing*. I considered it a booklet, but customers called it a book. It was also reviewed in major magazines and became an early bestseller for me.

One woman in that group of speakers heard me and thought, "I can write 16 pages."

Inspired, she started writing. She went beyond sixteen pages. A short time later she completed a full-length book. This one. You're holding it now. And it's outstanding.

That's the power of Cheryl Jones. She heard me speak and she took action. But the story doesn't stop there. She's also influenced me, too.

At another speaking event, I mentioned I was working on a book that I had not finished. In it, I talked about strongman training, where you learn to bend nails and horseshoes and do other "impossible" feats of strength. Cheryl was in that audience, too.

While I was talking, Cheryl blurted out, "I'd buy that book right now."

I stopped my presentation, stunned.

"Really?" I asked.

"Yes. I'd buy ten copies of it."

Because of her enthusiasm, I finished the book. It's called *Anything Is Possible*. And I gave Cheryl ten copies of it.

As you can see, she influenced me, and I influenced her. And the best news of all is, she can now influence you.

Her book is inspiring. And informative. A cheerleader and coach for your mind and soul. It's written clearly and shares tips, tricks and techniques you can use right now to have "Emotional Self Mastery."

Read it and turbocharge your life because Anything Is Possible!

Dr. Joe Vitale

www.MrFire.com

How to Get the Most from this Book

As you read this book, allow it to be a resource, a well-spring of possibilities from which to draw a refreshing drink. As harmful thoughts and emotions, negative self-talk, and undesired energy come into your awareness, use the tools within to help you deactivate and eliminate them from your psychic and energetic fields. Doing so regularly will decrease your negative reactions, build your self-confidence as a master of your emotions, and give you greater peace.

When you start cleaning up your thinking and eliminating negative emotions, you will begin to realize that you are more than your feelings. You'll more readily recognize your gifts, talents, hopes, and dreams. Your life will become a stark contrast to the life you previously lived. Magical things will begin to naturally happen as you neutralize the harmful negativity within. You start to live more from your heart, free from false beliefs and misinterpretations. Your everyday experience brightens. You'll feel more hopeful and will hold positive expectations for every situation. Good things will easily come your way.

I have applied and had success with every one of the techniques listed in this book. I've used them to neutralize a host of major and very common issues, such as fear of abandonment, self-judgment, lack of confidence, low self-esteem, poor spelling, low self-worth, constant complaining, frequent illness, headaches, and mild depression. Cleaning up my emotional and energetic fields has resulted in:

- Increased self-awareness

- Self-acceptance

- Greater self-confidence

- Living more authentically

- Self-assuredness

- Feeling comfortable in my own skin

- Increased polite-assertiveness

- Additional ideal clients

- More enjoyable work

- Greater passion in my relationship

- Increased appreciation of others

- Improved patience and understanding

- Loving relationships with my children

- Achievement of goals

- More laughter and joy

- Greater personal peace

What I have learned is that quite often one specific technique will be the perfect antidote for the pain or frustration you are experiencing. At other times, that same technique may not be as effective. If this occurs, simply try a different one. However, before you implement any of the methods, take a few moments to clearly define the feeling, the pain, or the issue as best you can. One of the best ways to force yourself to be clear is to describe the issue in writing, and then list all the feelings and thoughts associated with the issue. Describing it in written form will force you to use precise language. The more precise you are, the more effective the technique, and the better the results.

As you read the chapters that follow, you will find that each chapter includes a story. The story is intended to put the technique in context of how it may be used. Most stories also include the results the person achieved by using the technique, so you can know what kind of outcome you might expect. Of course, results vary. You may receive something even better than what the person in the story received. Two common reports from those working with these techniques include that their confidence soared, and they reported feeling "calm." As they became more self-aware and became a master of their emotions fewer things bothered them, they felt happier more often.

From personal experience, I can tell you that since I started dissolving my own negative emotions and limiting thoughts, barriers, and beliefs, I feel more positive, confident, and in control of my life. Resolving the persistent, unsupportive assumptions and self-talk caused me to feel that there were more possibilities than ever before. I've also noticed an increase in the number of wonderful opportunities coming my way since I started improving my emotional state and my thinking.

These techniques have positively influenced my perspective of the world and my place in it. They have helped bring me out of a pattern of self-doubt, depression and despair. Today, I feel optimistic, hopeful and happy ninety-eight percent of the time. Because these tools were so effective, I continue to use them regularly to maintain a positive attitude and a feeling of joy. It is because these tools worked so well for me that I truly believe they will work well for you, too.

Are you ready to master your emotions and feel enough? Let's get started!

Introduction
Mastering Your Emotions

As Pollyanna as it may sound, my mission in life is to bring greater peace to the world, one person at a time. When I say, *peace*, I mean *peace* within an individual, organization, or business so that each can contribute fully and joyfully.

Cultivating personal peace and ultimately, personal power and confidence, is challenging when we live in a society that continually fuels self-doubt and destroys self-esteem with criticism, bullying, and blatant disrespect. We witness ugliness in politics and in corporations. In business, employees spontaneously throw one another under the bus just to divert the boss' attention. Cultivating personal peace begins with learning to reclaim your own power and self-confidence through emotional self-mastery. Becoming a master of your emotions means not only recognizing when you have been triggered but also means choosing how you will react and feel. Emotional self-mastery places you squarely in control of yourself, your feelings and your power.

At one time or another, everyone experiences feelings of frustration, hurt, helplessness and even self-pity. These negative feelings become problematic when they're experienced on a frequent or ongoing basis. Receiving regular verbal jabs or sarcastic quotes from a spouse, a parent, or coworker reinforces an individual's secret fear of unworthiness. The more the fear is reinforced, the more believable it becomes, and the more the individual starts to criticize herself.

The longer you allow negative thoughts and emotions to linger, the more you will convey the same negative energy to those around you. Experiencing emotions of a low vibration, like anger, guilt, or shame on a regular basis will draw similar negative energy to you. If this pattern continues for some time, you will find yourself stuck in a constant low vibrational state of harmful thoughts and unsupportive self-talk. When you are stuck in this kind of negative energy pattern, it undermines your confidence and causes you to act in ways that are not congruent with your true-self. Changing your thoughts, emotions, and self-talk is possible. It requires self-awareness and deliberate action to shift yourself to a higher vibrational frequency.

Shifting your thoughts and emotions is what this book is all about—innovative techniques to transform your thoughts, emotions, and self-talk out of the lower vibrational emotions such as sadness, helplessness, and anger, to the higher vibrational emotions of contentment, confidence, and optimism. This transition makes it easy to love your life again.

I recommend that you experiment with and practice these techniques regularly. Before you know it, you'll strengthen your control over your feelings and become a master of your emotions. You'll feel happier, more relaxed, and more joyful. You'll have more energy, excitement, and enthusiasm for all aspects of your life. Other positive people will gravitate toward you, while negative people will fall away.

Are you ready to experience more joy and happiness in your life? Is it time for the negativity in your life to get the heck out? Are you willing to take charge and master your emotions so you can live more balanced and free?

Great! I thought you would say—yes. Let's get started!

The Influence of a False Assumption
My Story

I believe that some of the very best teachers are those who have the first-hand experience of what they set out to teach. Therefore, I am sharing that which I know personally.

Negative thoughts and emotions, and how to change them, is a subject I know plenty about. From an early age, I struggled with self-defeating thoughts and emotions. My challenge began with an assumption formed right after my birth that I had been abandoned. That assumption led me to hold two core beliefs: I'm not good enough to be loved, and I must please others to receive love.

This may sound weird, but I can remember events from the day I was born. I don't mean the birth process, but events that happened in the hours following my birth. My arrival was difficult for my mother. To make matters worse, she was ill (with what, it is not clear). Adding to the challenge, she suffered a broken tailbone. The delivery, illness, and tailbone made it hard for her to care for me in the hours immediately following my birth. Because the nurses were concerned about my under-developed immune system, they quarantined me to the nursery for the first day and a half. During the time alone, surrounded by unfamiliar sounds and faces, I concluded that I had been abandoned. Unfortunately, this conclusion was not easily overwritten even after I was released to go home with my parents. Instead, the false assumption became subconscious programming that ultimately led to my fear of being left behind.

It wasn't until I was in my early twenties that I learned about the details surrounding my birth. I was working with a counselor to figure out why I continued to feel depressed, uneasy and generally disenchanted with my life. At that point, I should have been having a ball. I was in college. I was working, making enough money to pay bills and still play on the weekends. But I wasn't happy. The counselor invited me to try something called regression hypnotherapy. She explained that it was a little like hypnosis, but the client is totally aware throughout the process. I agreed, and we began. I was willing to try just about anything to feel better.

I don't remember the exact details of the process, but what I do remember is that I identified the main feeling as abandonment and her asking me to remember a time when I experienced that feeling. After I had located an event in my teen years, she asked me to find another event that was before the one I had just recalled. She continued to ask me to find an earlier and earlier event until I remembered the day I was born. I could recall each event as if it had taken place yesterday. I could see all the details in my mind. I could remember being in the nursery looking up at the fluorescent ceiling lights. I could see the sides of the plastic bassinet. I could recall thinking that no one was coming back for me. That was the day I began to write the story that I had been abandoned.

A day or so after meeting with the counselor, I visited my mother to ask her a few questions about the day I was born. Without prompting or suggestion, she shared that the day she went into labor, she was sick and was in a lot of pain. Because of all the complications, she was unable to care for me. She went on to explain that I spent a lot of time in the nursery as the doctors tried to get her infection and pain under control. This information validated what I recalled in therapy and explained my fear of abandonment but did not resolve the issues.

Even though I understood what caused the false belief, I didn't have the knowledge or skill to change my interpretation. Nor did I recognize how it influenced in my daily life.

I continued to struggle with the fear of not being enough and of being abandoned. These beliefs took a toll on my relationships and career. Holding these beliefs caused me to crave attention, to look for acknowledgment, and to live in a constant state of trying to please others. I read self-help books, went to counseling, and attended intensive workshops and retreats to try to resolve my problem. Gradually, things improved as I learned to master my emotions and release false beliefs.

My job today as a professional speaker, trainer, and personal coach affords me opportunities to work with individuals of all backgrounds and careers. Many of whom have shared their own stories of struggle. Those stories often echoed the experiences I faced at one time or another. Don't get me wrong. I don't believe that all these people suffer from abandonment. However, it is likely that they too carry false beliefs that have skewed their expectations of themselves and the world around them.

More than ever, people are acting out their unhappiness, frustration, and hurt. They find fault, fight with others, and engage in behavior that is self-sabotaging. They blame their boss, coworker, or spouse. They set low expectations for their own performance, avoid learning new skills, and wait for someone else to take the initiative. Then, they complain. They say they are mistreated and claim ethnic or gender bias. Yet, if they were to take an objective look inside their own minds, they would soon see the one treating them poorly, is themselves.

It begins within. When we learn and practice emotional self-mastery, we will live more peacefully and attract positivity into our lives. We also regain our personal power and self-confidence. And, who doesn't want that? Join me. Won't You? Turn the page to get started.

Section One
Emotional Self-Mastery Leads to Happiness

Emotional Self-Mastery Assessment

How well do you know yourself? I expect that you would say, "I know myself pretty well." But do you? Do you know yourself well enough to know what things trigger a negative emotional response within you? Are you able to recognize the thoughts that cause you grief? Many people are aware of *when* they get emotionally triggered, but few are aware of the thought patterns *behind* the triggers, which were actually the originating cause of their emotional discomfort.

Let's look at what may be triggering you. Think about your answers to these questions.

- Do the actions or words of others easily affect you emotionally?

- What do others do that causes you frustration or anger?

- Do you have a co-worker who drives you nuts?

- Does your boss, family member, or partner say things that get under your skin?

- Have you ever been told that you're "too sensitive"?

Take the following self-assessment to help you determine how often your emotions are running your life. It will also give you an idea of how well you manage your responses to negative triggers. Using a scale of 1 to 5, rate each statement to indicate how often you've experienced the feeling or scenario.

<u>Rating Scale</u>

1. 1 Frequently
2. 2 Often
3. 3 Occasionally
4. 4 Rarely
5. 5 Never

1. How often do you feel overwhelmed at work or at home?

2. With what frequency do you get irritated by the actions or attitudes of others?

3. How much of the time are you trying to make others happy?

4. How often do you fight or argue with a partner or a family member?

5. How frequently do you feel that your life or destiny is out of your control?

6. How often do you complain about family members, your partner, or work?

7. How much time do you spend telling others what's wrong with your life or relationship?

8. How frequently do you become defensive when others correct you?

9. How often have you been told that you wear your feelings on your sleeve or are too sensitive?

10. With what frequency do you feel like you'll explode in either anger or tears?

11. How often do you become mad at work?

12. How often do you criticize your appearance or your body?

13. How often have you hung on to an unhealthy relationship for fear of being alone or never finding someone else?

14. How often have you been involved with conflict or controversy at work, with neighbors, or with friends?

15. How often do you blame others for you not meeting expectations?

16. How frequently does teasing from co-workers or friends get under your skin?

17. How often do you lose your patience with a co-worker, boss, or family member?

18. How often have you had the thought that you are not living the life you deserve?

19. How often do you cut others off when they are talking?

20. How often do you worry about feeling rejected by someone important to you?

Your Emotional Self-Mastery Score

Total the points for each of your answers to determine your emotional self-mastery score:

80 or higher - **You're a Super Star!** – You have a high level of self-awareness and are likely on your way to emotional self-mastery. You are not easily triggered by the actions, words, and attitudes of others. You likely take the behavior of others in stride and not personally.

70 – 80 - **You're Better Than Most, Good Job!** – You have an above-average level of self-awareness and are making headway toward emotional self-mastery. Continue to stay conscious of your thoughts and assumptions, and recognize the role they play in triggering your emotions.

60 – 70 - **You're Doing OK, Could Be Better** – You are ripe for more happiness. There is room for increased self-awareness. You may want to make a list of the things that cause you the most frustration and apply the techniques in this book to learn how to avoid getting triggered so often.

60 or below - **You're Struggling, Aren't You?** – You are likely experiencing many emotions daily, and you may feel out of control at times. Be aware that your emotions may be a liability in your interpersonal relationships and could be causing you problems at work and home. You may want to seek professional assistance to dissolve the internal anger, hurt, or resentment that may be causing you frustration. The techniques you find within this book will help you get started. Good luck!

Emotions and Their Vibrational Frequencies

Albert Einstein is quoted as saying, "Everything is vibration." Through his research he discovered that all matter is actually energy vibrating at such a low frequency it appears as a solid. Everything has vibration, including emotions! Think about it, the emotion of sadness feels low and slow as compared to the emotion of joy, which feels high and light. The thing to remember is that the higher the vibrational frequency, the lighter you will feel physically, emotionally, and mentally. That vibrational quality is what we strive for—the experience of feeling light, bright, and vibrant.

What I find most interesting about the vibrational frequency of emotions is that there is a hierarchy. In 1984, Louise Hay published a book called *You Can Heal Your Life*. In it, she shares the hierarchy chart of the major emotions. She calls the chart "The Emotional Guidance System." On the chart each emotion is listed from the highest to the lowest vibrational frequency. Love, joy, and freedom are placed at the top of the list, with the highest vibrational frequency. Fear, grief, and powerlessness are at the bottom, with the lowest frequency.

Hay was not the only person to study and measure the frequencies of emotion. David R. Hawkins, M.D., Ph.D., also studied the vibrational qualities of emotions and published his findings in a book entitled *Power Vs. Force: The Hidden Determinants of Human Behavior*. Dr. Hawkins' study arrived at a slightly different outcome regarding the emotion with the lowest vibrational frequency. He identified shame as having a vibrational frequency lower than fear or guilt.

Since the time I was first exposed to this information in the late 1990s, I've continued to study and work with emotional vibrational frequencies to better understand their power and implications, especially as they affect the work environment. Over the past twenty years, I have used this information as a basis to help my clients determine the core issues behind self-sabotage and poor performance at work. These discoveries, along with the subsequent interventions that followed, have had some astonishing, if not miraculous, results.

Because I feel that both Hay's and Hawkins' work is equally powerful, I've developed an emotional hierarchy chart that provides the best of both authors. Below, I've merged the two charts and retested the order to provide you with a comprehensive picture of the scale of emotions.

Emotional Hierarchy Chart

The emotions listed here are in the order of vibrational frequency from highest to lowest.

1. Love, Joy, Empowerment, Freedom

2. Passion, Appreciation, Compassion

3. Enthusiasm, Eagerness, Belief

4. Positive Expectation

5. Optimism

6. Hope

7. Contentment
   _____

8. Boredom

9. Pessimism

10. Frustration, Irritation, Impatience

11. Overwhelm

12. Disappointment

13. Doubt

14. Worry

15. Blame

16. Discouragement

17. Anger

18. Revenge

19. Hatred, Rage

20. Insecurity, Guilt, Unworthiness

21. Fear, Grief

22. Powerlessness, Shame

When you review the chart, you will notice that high frequency emotions such as, joy, gratitude, love, appreciation, passion, optimism, hopefulness, and contentment define the upper limits of emotional vibration. Meanwhile, emotions such as worry, blame, discouragement, anger, revenge, hatred, guilt, fear, powerlessness, and shame fill out the lowest portion of the chart. Powerlessness and shame produce the lowest levels of vibration.

You can think of the emotional hierarchy chart as a ladder leading to the highest and most desirable state of being, defined as enlightenment. When you resonate at the frequency of enlightenment, you have reached nirvana—the frequency all human life strives to obtain. If enlightenment is the destination the ladder leads you to, that would make love and joy the highest step on the ladder before enlightenment.

Working our way up from the bottom, the rung closest to the bottom is powerlessness and shame. The next step up is fear and grief. The rungs in between those at the bottom and those at the top hold all the other emotions at varying frequencies as their vibrations increase from the bottom.

What I have learned from working with the emotional hierarchy chart is that it's extremely difficult to leap from rung one (shame) up to rung four (revenge). You must do the necessary work before you can climb your energy up the ladder. You must take incremental steps, usually moving one rung at a time to a place that feels a bit better. On occasion, you might think that you've jumped several rungs to a much higher level, like leaping from discouragement to frustration. Often the jump is because you've had a surge in your energy due to an outside influence. In those cases, the jump is usually short-lived. In my experience, it was due to large amounts of espresso consumed in a day, but those "better feeling" emotions couldn't last, no matter how much caffeine I consumed. However, the exercises contained within this book are designed to help you raise your vibrational frequency in a way that allows you to sustain a higher vibration.

One more thing about the chart. You'll notice a line drawn between contentment and boredom. This is the line of neutrality, the midway point of emotions. Emotions above that line are considered positive or higher frequency emotions. Those below are considered negative and lower frequency. Our goal is to stay in the emotions that are above the line as much as possible.

Regularly experiencing above-the-line emotions has many benefits. Higher frequency emotions add to your emotional and physical health, help you feel good about self, increase your self-confidence, and build emotional resilience. Conversely, spending too much time below the line drains your emotional reserves; adds strain and stress on your relationships; and negatively impacts your emotional, physical, and mental wellbeing.

You can feel more resilient by living in a higher-frequency emotional state, which means experiencing optimism, enthusiasm, excitement, and joy—often. Maintaining emotions that are on the higher end of the scale results in increased flexibility and feelings of appreciativeness and gratitude. A byproduct of living at the high end is the ability to bounce back quickly from adverse situations. The more resilient you are, the faster you recover from unexpected negative interactions. Additionally, when you increase your emotional resilience, you are triggered less frequently by other people's odd behavior. Wouldn't that be nice?

From personal experience, I can honestly say that the things that once triggered me are far fewer than they used to be. Seven years ago, it didn't take much for me to get upset, feel sorry for myself, or make someone else responsible for the way I was feeling. Today, it's an entirely different story. There are very few situations that occur in my life today that result in me getting upset or blaming others. In fact, I can't think of a time in recent memory where I felt angry or hurt for more than ten to fifteen minutes. It is really quite nice to be living above-the-line on the emotional frequency chart. (Of course, I'm not quite yet to enlightenment!) I think I'll stay here. Won't you join me?

Emotional Self-Mastery and Happiness

One field of study on happiness suggests that the average person's happiness is based on a 50-10-40 breakdown. This popular positive psychology theory states that your level of happiness is determined by three things in varying amounts: 50 percent by your genetics, 10 percent by your circumstances, 40 percent by your actions, attitudes, and the way you respond to circumstances. I emphatically disagree with this theory. With the exception of individuals who have a clinical psychological issue, I believe that the average person's influence over their personal happiness is well over 80 percent.

Personal experience, observation, and working one-on-one with hundreds of people to change their experiences has led me to believe that 80 percent of our happiness is based on: 1) how we interpret events and interactions; 2) how we add meaning to our interpretation; and 3) how we respond emotionally. The remaining 20 percent may be influenced by genetics, but also by chemical and hormonal fluctuations within the body, as well as by the foods and beverages we choose to ingest. The point is that we each have the capacity and responsibility to choose happiness instead of blaming our genetics or circumstances. Here's why.

Let's say that Jo, your best friend at work, was just promoted to a position that you had also applied and interviewed for. It was a position you thought you had in the bag based on your tenure with the company. What would be your immediate reaction?

You might say, "Good for him. I'm so glad he got the position. He'll make a great supervisor." Or your response might be, "What the heck? I'm more qualified than he is. I've been here longer. What were they thinking?"

Then, what would your follow-up conversation with yourself have been? Would you have listed why Jo shouldn't have gotten the job? Would you have gone into all the reasons you were a more suitable pick? Would you have made excuses about your performance during the interview? Would you have blamed the hiring manager, insisting that he or she was wrong, unfairly favored Jo, or was a poor judge of character?

What would you have said to yourself *about* yourself? Would you have made one of these statements to yourself? "I'm never chosen for the good jobs? No one ever notices how hard I work. No one appreciates what I do around here."

You see, for every significant experience (good or bad), we take the facts, make an interpretation, and then add meaning to what happened, and that becomes our story. Some of our stories are based purely in fact, while other aspects of it are sheer conjecture. An experience or message from someone outside ourselves without interpretation is just that—an experience or a message. The stories with little or no meaning added are the ones we tend to forget. Because these events weren't deemed significant enough or weren't tied to a previous belief or emotion, they don't tend to get archived in our memory.

Meaningful stories are stories we unconsciously pay attention to, recall regularly, and operate from throughout our lives. Unfortunately, many of these seemingly *meaningful* stories have a strong connotation. We know this because they are typically based in limitation or negativity. Unfortunately, they can cause us harm without us realizing it. Before I became aware of their influence, these stories surreptitiously coaxed me into believing that I didn't measure up; I wasn't enough. These beliefs caused me to think that I had to work twice as hard as anyone else and that I wasn't fine just the way I was. In addition, those same stories convinced me that I couldn't become who I dreamt of being.

During my late teens and early twenties, I had a personal library fully stocked with these kinds of false stories—most of which came from well-meaning parents, grandparents, and teachers trying to set me straight with "realistic" expectations based on their own shortcomings and limited beliefs. One such message came into being during my junior year of high school. Arriving home after school one afternoon, I announced to my parents that I planned to study oceanography because I wanted to save the dolphins. My enthusiasm was met with a dose of grown-up reality, "You can't be an oceanographer, you're terrible at math. The sciences require too much math. You need to find a career that doesn't require math." The message was clear; I didn't have what they thought was necessary to be an oceanographer. Nor did they think I would be able to get there.

Flippant remarks like that and others validated already present beliefs within—"I am imperfect" and "I am not enough"—which led to beliefs of incapability and self-doubt. Reflecting on that experience with greater awareness, I realize that most of those messages had more to do with the person who spoke them and what they thought was possible for themselves than they had to do with me. How could those people have possibly known what I would be capable of: a multi-unit restaurant manager, a food cost controller, business owner, speaking professional, an author? Who knew?

To illustrate the process of how messages are morphed into emotions and then into beliefs, I devised this diagram.

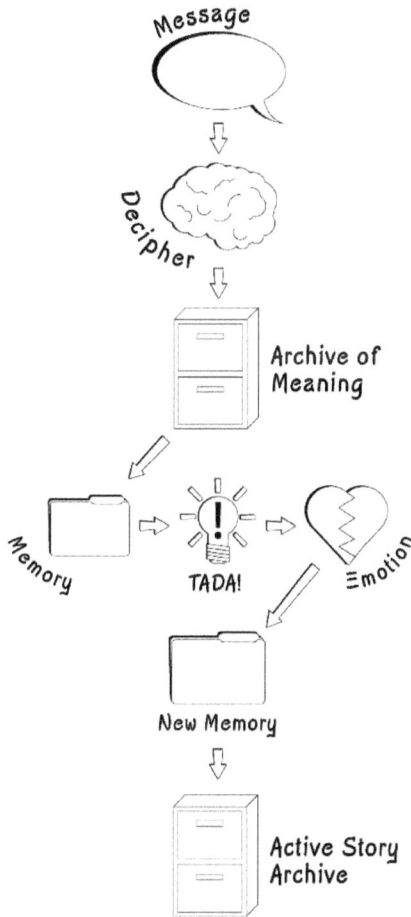

Illustration by Blake Griffin

Imagine a message is sent to you. It comes to you in one of these forms: verbal, written, or through body language. Your brain receives the message.

Upon receipt, the message has no meaning. It's nothing more than a bunch of sounds, scribbles, or gestures. Once the message sinks in, the brain prepares to decipher it and add meaning.

For your brain to give the message meaning, it must explore the archives of your memory to find some experience, knowledge, or information that will help you make sense of it. Once it does, it creates a link to the prior information and meaning, forms an association, and ta-da, your message now has meaning.

A message's meaning (the meaning you give it) is what triggers your emotions. When the meaning activates a negative experience or false belief that you already have stored in your archives about yourself, it causes you to experience low vibration emotions. If the low vibration emotions are strong enough, or are repeatedly activated, it can cause the emotion and story to be filed in your active story archive.

The active story archive is the reference section of your internal library. It's the place where you've collected and categorized your life stories along with their meanings. The active story archive is what tells you how you relate to everything else in the world and how you fit in. It can also give you a sense of who you are. It's important to know this, because each time you enter a new situation, your brain attempts to reference a similar situation in your active story archive. Then, when it finds one, the brain says, "Aha, I know what this means and how it relates to me."

Ponder this. The "N-word" is considered one of the most highly offensive words in the English language. Yet, I want you to imagine that you have no association to this word; pretend that you have never heard it before. Now, let's assume that you overheard a conversation in which the word is used several times with no extra emphasis placed on it. Do you think you would feel offended? My guess is no, probably not. You would likely not feel anything at all. It would be like hearing a word in an unfamiliar language—it would have no *meaning* to you. A word or a message has no power until you add meaning to it.

The brain always looks for a connection in your active story archive, before it looks for an alternative explanation. The unfortunate part is that your archive has flaws, and those flaws can mislead you. While many of your archived stories will provide you with a sense of comfort and stability, others may have a false storyline, causing you to feel threatened, fearful, or inferior. If you've ever felt like you were stuck in a pattern of feeling down, it may have been due to the active stories in your archive. The good news is that you hold in your hands the power to change any unwanted pattern.

Earlier, we talked about emotions as energy. If you have ever seen a child having a tantrum, or if you can remember having one yourself (maybe even as recently as last week) you know there is a lot of energy involved. Intense emotions produce an energy field around you. That field expands out beyond your physical body. Do you remember the character, Pigpen, from the Charles Schultz's Peanuts cartoons? Wherever Pigpen traveled, he was engulfed by a cloud of dirt and dust. Pigpen's cloud is like your energy field. Wherever you go, it goes. Pigpen's cloud could be seen. Yours can't be seen, but it can be *sensed* by others. Have you have ever walked into a room where two people have just been arguing and felt tension in the air? When your energy field is filled with negative emotions, it's no secret to those around you, even when you try to cover it up.

The same is true regarding positive emotions. You have surely experienced walking into a room where people were celebrating or laughing. That room likely felt warm and inviting. Energy that is light and energetic is such a pleasure. It feels good to be there and it may cause you to stay longer.

When I speak of emotional self-mastery, I'm defining it as the ability to *choose* how you react and ultimately feel in any given moment, regardless of the conditions. It is about becoming aware of and changing your response to internal and external stimuli that cause you to respond in an emotional way. We're not talking about the stimuli that cause you to feel positive emotions like hope, joy, and happiness. Self-mastery is about gaining control over your reactions to the triggers that cause negative emotions, such as sadness, fear, rage—anything other than feeling good. More simply stated, emotional self-mastery is managing and minimizing the effects of negative triggers.

As you begin to develop greater emotional self-mastery, you will notice that the triggers of the past have less and less strength. Previously powerful triggers won't hold the punch they once did. As you learn and practice the skills that I've outlined, you'll further develop your ability to sense, shift, and maintain a positive awareness. You'll learn to get and stay emotionally balanced. The daily roller coaster of emotions you once experienced will subside and you will no longer be a victim of your circumstances. Your triggers will weaken, and you'll be triggered less often by the actions of others. Instead, you'll feel happier, more hopeful, and in control of your emotions. Ultimately, you'll notice increased energy, more opportunities, and bounteous choices. Other byproducts include an increase in self-confidence and professional success. Emotional self-mastery is the key to a joyful and prosperous future.

In case you were wondering, emotional self-mastery is not about biting your tongue, holding your breath, or stuffing your emotions. Nor is it about putting on an indifferent, stoic face when you experience strong feelings. Instead, it's about recognizing that in every scenario you have the power to choose how you want to feel, and how you will interpret the events, as well as interpret the actions of others. You also get to decide what meaning those events will have for you, and for how long you will experience the energy connected to your meaning or interpretation.

Regularly choosing your emotions puts you on the path to emotional self-mastery. As you gain more control over your knee-jerk reactions of the past, you will find that you start living more freely, with greater passion and happiness—the freedom, passion, and happiness that you have always deserved.

Emotions and Your Biochemistry

E motions produce a waterfall of chemical reactions in the body that impact the normal functioning of your biological system. Each time you have a thought, negative or positive, it results in a chemical release event that produces an electrochemical reaction within your body.

Here's what we know about the connection between emotions and the body. In the 1980s, the scientific community's concept of how the human body works was challenged when a group of researchers, including molecular biologist and author of *Molecules of Emotion*, Candice Pert, and others, proved that thoughts and emotions cause distinct neuron firing patterns within the brain, which coincided with chemical releases throughout the body. These radically thinking scientists were able to prove the connection between the many systems of the human body. They showed that no single system operates separate from any other, and that our thoughts and emotions play a significant role in our overall health and well-being.

Your Thoughts Change Your Brain

N ewsflash! In case you didn't know it, I'm here to tell you that every single minute of every day the thoughts you repeatedly think are programming your mind and influencing the chemical functions of your body.

You may be thinking, "What? My thoughts are impacting my body? No way!"

Yes, way! Just like the more frequently you practice an activity—singing, dancing, golfing, speaking a foreign language—the easier it becomes. You've done it. You know it's true. The more often you move your body in a specific pattern, the more it becomes ingrained in your muscle memory. The same is true of the thoughts you think. When you think a thought over and over, it forges a neural pathway in your brain. Done often enough, that pathway becomes the go-to path for any thoughts of a similar nature.

Think of it like this. You're taking a walk along a paved walkway in the woods and all of sudden you notice a narrow trail off to the right. It's too narrow for human foot-traffic, but the perfect width for deer to travel. While you are noticing this trail, you notice something else—the path is well worn. Here's a clue. The more worn down the vegetation is on the trail, the more often that trail has been used by local wildlife. That trail is like a neural pathway in your brain. The more frequently you think a thought, the more worn-in it becomes in your brain. Like trails in the wild, the more worn the path, the easier it is to travel. Information, true or false, would rather travel along the easiest path, the one with the least resistance.

What you may not know is that your repetitive thoughts and snap judgments of yourself (and others) cause a sequence of unseen events to occur within your body. Each time you think a negative or limiting thought about yourself or another, you release a series of chemicals into your bloodstream. These chemical messengers, called neuropeptides, surge through your body searching for compatible receptors to hook up to. After a suitable receptor is found, they hook up and lock on. Once they've locked on, a chemical interaction occurs. It's like turning a key, causing a change to the structure of that cell.

But wait! There's more! All the fun doesn't end here. When the structure of the cell changes, it sends a message to the entire body, causing it to respond in any number of ways. You might notice a surge of adrenaline causing you to want to fight or flee. Or you might notice your legs and hands shaking in response to a perceived threat.

Another interesting fact is that once a cell is changed, it stays changed. Which means that when it reproduces, or divides, it doubles the number of cells with that specific receptor. This becomes a problem when the reproducing cells have been hit by negativity. Negative thoughts, negative emotions, negative circumstances, all have the ability to change a cell. The cells that have been changed by negativity will produce more cells predestined to receive peptide messengers laced with negativity. This continues to generate cells prone to receive negative peptides rather than positive ones, unless…wait for it…we ***interrupt*** the cycle.

Historically researchers believed that cells in the human body replaced themselves every seven years. New studies reveal that some cells are never renewed or replaced, for example, those in the cerebral cortex. Cells in the cerebral cortex are unlike other parts of the body. What you are born with is what you have, when it comes to cerebral cortex cells. On the other hand, colon cells, along with skin cells, regenerate every four to five days, resulting in an entirely new skin in two to three weeks. Fascinating stuff! Isn't it?

Even though some cells are dying off and being replaced with new ones, it does not mean that they are unaffected by past releases of neurochemicals. Cells that have been influenced by chemical messengers from a barrage of negative thoughts or emotional trauma may have been compromised. Those impacted cells are now making new cells that match their current makeup. This means they are reproducing themselves as compromised cells, not as uninfluenced, brand new ones. The reproduction of compromised cells perpetuates an imbalance within the body.

Science has shown that neuropeptides are released with each thought we have, and those peptides can trigger certain desires and emotions. Thoughts, with their coinciding emotions, heavily influence the chemical releases in the body. These chemical reactions influence and control every bodily function, from thinking to digestion.

Studies over the past ten years have validated the influence of thoughts on the body. One such study was conducted in 2006 by Carol Look, a clinical psychotherapist, hypnotherapist, and Emotional Freedom Technique (EFT) master. Look's study focused on improving the vision of those who wore glasses by teaching them to release negative emotions, such as fear, anger, and guilt. Spanning a period of eight weeks, Look asked participants to follow a routine of releasing negative emotions using EFT. Prior to the start of the program, participants were asked to complete a questionnaire regarding their eyesight, lifestyle, and demographic background. Each week, the participants received written instructions on how to tap on certain points of the body to release a specific type of emotion. Participants tracked their progress and recorded the changes they observed as they continued the program. As a result, a significant number of people, 75 percent, reported that their eye sight had improved by the end of the study. That is just one clear example of how your thoughts can change your brain, or in this case, eyesight. To see the study protocol and the entire report with results, visit:

https://issuu.com/edu178/docs/improve_your_eyesight_with_eft_-_ca.

Section Two
Changing the Head Games

In this section, we will begin to explore techniques that can influence our negative patterns of thinking. You know what I'm talking about. Those patterns of self-doubt, negative self-talk, and put-downs. You will discover tools to forever change that kind of behavior. Are you ready? Let's Do This!

Technique #1: The Story Manager – Who's Running Your Life?

"We can change the story we tell ourselves… and by doing that, we change the future."
~ Eleanor Brown, The Weird Sisters

For weeks, Sarah had been looking forward to attending a once-in-a-lifetime concert by her favorite artist. She had spent what seemed like a fortune on two, third-row seats for herself and her best friend. She even decided to purchase a new outfit to wear to the show. The day of the show, Sarah received a text message from her best friend canceling on the concert. The friend made some lame excuse about *not feeling* like going. Sarah was devastated.

Up until that moment, she had fantasized about the fun they would have together, singing at the top of their lungs and dancing in the aisles. As soon as she read the message, she said to herself, "I should have known this was going to happen. She's done this to me before. I should know by now that I can't count on her to follow through. Why do I bother to invite her to things that are this important?" Sarah's heart was broken. She moped around the room for an hour, feeling disappointed and betrayed. Because this was a reoccurring pattern, Sarah was questioning the value of her friendship and she was taking her friend's flaky behavior very personally.

In the background, Sarah's thoughts ran an inside story. The tale included storylines of, "I can't count on people. They don't keep their word. They'll promise to be there, but then flake-out. People always let me down. This kind of thing always happens to me. I must protect myself from disappointment, because someone will pull the plug and kill my enthusiasm. I feel like a fool."

When Sarah and I met for her first coaching session, she shared the concert story with me and expressed how angry, disappointed, and hurt she felt. She complained about how lame her friend was and said she needed to find a new best friend—one she could count on or at least who treated her with the same respect she gave.

As she told the story, I waited for her to take a breath so as to not interrupt. Then I asked, "Who's running your story here? You or your story manager?"

Sarah looked at me, puzzled. "Story manager?" she asked.

I said, "Yes. You've developed a big story around this friend and what her actions mean about you. Do you see that?"

Sarah responded, "No, I don't see that. Tell me what you mean."

I explained that each of us has a story manager living within us. The story manager is an invisible guy or gal who watches and captures every event and interaction you have, and then creates a story about it by adding meaning. Then he or she archives the story in the appropriate category for your reference later. I went on to say, "It sounds as though your story manager has taken this story regarding the concert, melded it with a few others, and added some meaning like *disrespect* and *betrayal*. When a similar feeling occurs, the story manager retrieves all the previous similar stories that have a similar theme and parades them in front of you, reinforcing the belief that you've been disrespected or betrayed."

Sarah said, "Holy cow! I never thought of it like that. I can see how that makes sense and how those stories are making me feel bad. What can I do to shut down the story manager?

Applying the Story Manager Technique

The purpose of the story manager technique is to separate fact from fiction when it comes to the events of our lives. Every significant story of our lives has both some facts and some fiction. The facts are usually pretty obvious. They are things like "It was raining," "My clothes got wet," or "My feet slipped." The fictional portion of a story is the inferences or meanings added to the facts, like "It's always gloomy on my birthday," "My bad luck ensured that I would get soaked," or "I'm unstable on my feet."

The stories the story manager makes up are often based on facts that have been twisted into a different reality. When we place those stories under a magnifying glass, we often see an underlying unmet need or belief. For instance, in the scenario of the rain falling on a birthday, the truth is that no matter when rain falls, it is on someone's birthday. It doesn't fall because it is *your* birthday. The added meaning is not true.

If you start to listen objectively to the stories you tell yourself, you will likely notice how the story has been embellished. You can use this technique to help you separate facts from fiction when you feel heavy, deflated, or depressed.

1. Notice the feeling. Locate the place in your body where you feel a heaviness or undesired emotion. For instance, Sarah mentioned feeling "heartbroken." She might look to her heart for answers.

2. Give the story manager a face. Close your eyes and imagine that you are standing in a huge library with stacks of books lined up in rows, one after the other. Behind the reference desk is the story manager.

    a) What does the story manager look like?

    b) How do you perceive him or her? Helpful? Careful? Scared? Small? Powerless? What words would you use to describe him or her?

    c) What were the specific facts of the situation?

    d) What meaning was added to the facts?

    e) What message is the story manager trying to give you?

    f) What story is he/she telling you about this situation? In Sarah's case, with the friend, the story manager was cautioning her, trying to help her avoid getting hurt. The story later expanded into "there was something wrong with Sarah." That message was not true nor was it part of the facts.

3. Ask yourself how you would *prefer* to feel: Happy? Excited? Joyful? Delighted?

4. What does the story manager *want* from you? Does she want reassurance? Security? To avoid disappointment? To be in control?

5. Imagine asking the story manager what action you need to take for both of you to have what you need. In Sarah's case, she recognized two things. First, she realized her happiness didn't depend on what her friend did or didn't do. She could be excited and joyful with or without her best friend along. Second, she realized that it is a good idea to have a backup plan when including that friend in an invitation. Ultimately, Sarah acknowledged that her friend's cancellation had nothing to do with Sarah herself or her value as a person.

The story manager will always be with you, adding meaning to and cataloging experiences. The *meaning* that you allow him or her to give an experience is up to you. You get to decide. What is important for you to know is that the story manager is always there, working behind the scenes. If you don't decide what meaning will be given to an experience or interaction, the story manager will.

Anytime you feel a strained relation with a partner, friend, or colleague, be sure to revisit the facts of the situation to separate the made-up portion from the reality. That made-up portion isn't the truth. Remember, when fictional data is added to facts, it changes the meaning. Stay alert to the facts of the story and take a moment to separate facts from fiction. When you do you'll have a cleaner, more positive library of experiences to choose from in the future.

Technique #2: The Story Manager Reboot

"You are the author of your life.
You create the story and you can rewrite it."
~ Fabienne Fredrickson

As you have just learned, the story manager is alive within you and has been placing meaning on your life events since before you were born. As a result, you likely have quite a few stories stored in your archives. The question is, what can you do about those unsupportive interpretations of past events? May I offer you a solution? I call it the story manager reboot.

When you reboot a computer, you restart it, giving the hardware and software a chance to reorganize the internal workings of the programing. When you reboot the story manager, you draft a new edition of the story, giving it a new meaning. The facts stay the same, but the end result interpretation can be empowering and helpful.

The story manager reboot is about you taking on the role of Story Manager and reclaiming the story for good instead of evil. (I know—I'm starting to sound a bit like a screenplay writer. But hang in there with me.) Wouldn't you agree that the unsupportive stories have been the antagonist of your personal story? So, why not reboot them to make you the hero instead? It boils down to you changing the meaning associated with the event. Simple as that. Here's how.

Applying the Story Manager Reboot Technique

Teri grew up in a household where her mother told her that she was "no good and would never amount to anything." One of the first times her mother made such a comment was when Teri tried to surprise her mother by making pasta for dinner. Unfortunately, she overcooked it and it turned mushy. Instead of expressing appreciation for the effort, her mother made jokes and comments about how Teri better marry a man who could cook because her cooking was no good. From her mother's teasing, Teri's story manager created a message that Teri was a bad cook, and she would succeed only if she found a husband who could cook.

To use the story manager reboot technique, Teri would need to remember the facts of the situation. Here are the facts she could recall: Mother wasn't feeling well. I wanted to help and show I could do it. I wanted to make dinner for mother and dad. I was excited to try. I was sure I could do it, because I had watched her do it in the past. I got distracted by the dog and forgot that the pasta was cooking. As a result, the pasta was mushy. Mother joked at my lack of cooking skills, suggesting I couldn't cook for a husband.

Now let's reboot the story with an empowering message.

At age eight, Teri wanted to help her mother, who wasn't feeling well that day. She was sure that she could make pasta because she had seen her mother do it many times. At some point during the cooking process, Teri got distracted by the dog and forgot about the pasta cooking on the stove. When she returned and poured the water off, the pasta was mushy. That day Teri learned that, when cooking pasta, she might want to set a timer to remind her of how long to cook it and to stay close by to check it regularly. Because of her pasta-making experience as a child, Teri now makes the best pasta.

A reboot takes the facts of the story and reworks them to have a positive meaning and outcome. In Teri's story, the pasta was still mush in the rewrite, but the negative portions of the story were reinterpreted to give it a positive outcome. Try this technique to allow the new story to overwrite a previous negative one in the archives. Tell the new story to yourself several times, until it becomes the *first* thought that comes to mind when you remember this topic.

Technique #3: Journaling for Insight

"Journal writing is a voyage to the interior."
~ Christina Baldwin

Like many teenagers in the 1970s, I struggled to figure out who I was and how to fit in to a culture that didn't seem to be mine. Matters were made more difficult by the fact that I was highly sensitive to the energy of others. I was, and still am, an empath and an intuitive woman. I feel and see things other people don't even notice.

Because I was sensitive to other's energy and emotions, I tended to pick up their thoughts and feelings as my own. I might feel sad or upset on any given day and not know why. There were times when I knew something bad was about to happen but was afraid to tell anyone for fear that they would think I was crazy. Then when the exact event occurred as I predicted, I would feel responsible and devastated that I did nothing to intervene. It was a heavy burden to carry as teenager.

The ongoing surge of information and emotions I took on from others caused a lot of internal confusion. As a result, my sense of self got jumbled up by all the outside influences. It would be years before I developed the ability to distinguish my thoughts and energy from that of others. The energetic confusion paired with a low self-esteem caused me to feel unimportant and small.

During this same chaotic period, my parents were having their own difficulties. Unknown to me, their relationship had been on the rocks for years. They had finally decided to separate when I was fourteen years of age and would eventually divorce. This was a challenging period for me; my relationship with my father was strained and became more so after he flippantly responded to my request to spend more time together by saying, "Cheryl, you remind me too much of your mother. I can't be around you right now." That statement landed like a crushing blow to my head *and* heart. Heartbroken, I needed a way to process my shock and profound sadness. Journaling provided a way to gain clarity and perspective during that difficult time.

My journals became my best friend—a place to reveal my thoughts and feelings without judgment or correction from an authority figure telling me how I *should* feel. I could be myself, truthful and honest. The pages were a place to rant, scream, and cry out my sadness and rage. Many angry words hit the pages of my journal. Once I got past a good portion of the pain, the pages started to hold descriptions of unfulfilled wishes, desires, and fantasies. When one book was filled, I'd move on to another. I still have the journals from my teens as a reminder of the distance I've come. And I still make a regular practice of journaling today.

I'm not the only one journaling these days. There seems to be a resurgence of people journaling. They meet in small groups or work independently. I have noticed a slow and steady increase in the number of folks who say they regularly journal. I often hear people reference the book, *The Artist's Way*, by Julia Cameron and Mark Byron, as their inspiration for taking up writing again.

The Artist's Way was one of the first books to provide specific techniques for journaling. Cameron suggests journaling as a method to "nurture your creative side." We spend the majority of our time working in our logical left brain. As we complete tasks necessary to manage work and home life, we neglect our creative right brain. It rarely gets to come out to play. To help nurture the right brain, Cameron suggests setting aside time each day to write. She encourages us to write three pages a day, long-hand instead of typing, to allow the body to be fully involved in the process. She coaches to write without judgment of handwriting or content. Allow whatever wants to come out on the pages to do so without hesitation. Even if no specific idea surfaces, keep writing. Eventually something of value will come out.

I still journal, but there are those days when there seems to be nothing to write about. At those moments, I insert a question to consider. Questions are some of the best writing prompts. They help you gain insight and understanding. Here are twenty prompts to get you started.

Journaling Prompts

1. What scares me the most? Why?

2. What do I dream of doing?

3. What makes me most happy?

4. What are my top three personal values? Define each of them.

5. What one thing, if changed, would help me experience more happiness every day?

6. What do I like about myself?

7. What are my best characteristics?

8. What makes my heart feel fulfilled?

9. How have I grown over the past year?

10. What do I love about my work?

11. Where have I let myself down in the past? What can I do to recover from it?

12. What is most important to me? Why?

13. Where do I want my life to head from this point on?

14. What emotions would I prefer to experience on a regular basis?

15. What made-up story do I have that could be rewritten with a new outcome?

16. What do I have to lose by speaking my truth and living authentically?

17. How has my family of origin influenced my choices and assumptions about myself?

18. What beliefs are holding me back from achieving my dreams?

19. If I had no limitations, I would start doing _____, today?

20. If you could have a casual conversation with anyone living or dead, who would it be and what would you talk about?

Applying the Journaling Technique

1. Sit quietly where you will have few interruptions or distractions.

2. Take a couple of deep cleansing breaths with your eyes closed to help center yourself.

3. Focus on the center of your chest. Get in touch with your heart center.

4. With your eyes still closed, state one of the prompts from the list above, several times, out loud or silently in your head. Allow yourself several minutes to contemplate the prompt before you begin to write.

5. Write freely without editing. Capture what enters your mind. Follow the rabbit trail, where ever it may go. Record ideas, sentence fragments, bullet points, images, single words, whatever is generated by the topic. Your writing doesn't need to make sense or even be in complete sentences.

6. When you are finished, close your journal entry with a statement of gratitude. Consider acknowledging the pages with, "Thank you for these pages and the gift they are to me."

Technique #4: Cancel, Cancel!
That's Not the Truth

"When you become conscious of your thoughts you will gain power over them."
~ Cheryl C. Jones

C an you remember the last time you thought about your thoughts? I know, it sounds funny to ask about *thinking*, but one of the most powerful ways to change the way you *feel* is to change what you *think*.

Without knowing it, you have developed patterns of repetitive thought, many of which are negative or limiting in nature. Unfortunately, frequent statements repeated in your head create a rut in your thinking. Repetitive thoughts like, "I'll never be able to lose the weight," become your new truth. After a short while, your thoughts gravitate toward the rut because it is so worn in; it becomes the route of least resistance.

To change rutted thinking you must change the input data. Just like with a computer, if you are programming and are not getting the outcome you were expecting, you must reconsider the data you're inputting. Bad data *in* results in bad data *out*.

Let's say that we were to identify bad data and change it to something better, more accurate. Then we might get a different outcome, right? Taking our weight loss example above, let's say the bad data that had been going in said, "It's too hard to lose ten pounds." To change the bad data, we need to know the truth or at least a more accurate statement to replace it with. That statement might be, "Weight loss is an incremental process. One pound at a time."

Additionally, you need to let the system know to stop processing the prior information-pack. It's like clicking the "End Task" button on your PC. (Sorry, Mac users.) To end the processing of the old information, you say to yourself, "Cancel, cancel. That is not the truth." Then you follow it with a truer, more accurate statement.

Here are a few examples of how you might reframe your thoughts around some popular topics.

- It's too hard to lose the extra fifteen pounds. I'll never be able to do it.

    o Replace with: Weight loss is a slow, steady process. To ensure that the weight stays off, I'll practice patience with myself and speak loving messages to my reflection in the mirror.

- I'll never get rid of this fat around my waist.

    o Replace with: My waist is getting thinner. Today, I commit to walking around my neighborhood. Tomorrow, I'll commit again to doing the same.

- It's too late for me to change careers.

    o Replace with: I wonder how many credits it would take to get my master's degree? It would feel so good to have my degree.

- I'll never be as successful as I want to be.

    o Replace with: I'm going to define success and determine what steps I need to take to reach it.

- Will I ever be able to write that book? It's an overwhelming task.

    o Replace with: Author Joe Vitale's first book was sixteen pages. I can write at least that many pages about a thing I'm passionate about.

- I'm not good enough, skilled enough, knowledgeable enough to _____.

    o Replace with: (Your turn now. How could you rewrite this one?)

- I'm too old to start a new business.

    o Replace with: (What could you write here?)

You're probably getting the picture now of how our thoughts can shoot us in the foot before we ever get started. And thinking those thoughts regularly can shut down our ability to learn new things, take on a new position, listen to ideas. I know because I've been there more times than I care to admit. The length of time it took me to write this book is just one example of my thoughts running roughshod over my good intentions. When I started this project, I was fairly clear on my goal. I had a dozen or so techniques that I knew worked well, and I wanted to share them with people like you who could use them. So, it shouldn't be any big deal for me to pull them all together to share with you, right? Wrong. Before this book was in this format, it took on many fits and starts. I realized that I couldn't complete the book until I canceled out the majority of my limiting and unsupportive thinking. However, not all of it went away. Some of that rutted thinking still pops into my brain from time to time. But, in the end, I won out over the thought machine.

To reprogram rutted thinking patterns like, "I'm not good enough, I don't fit in, I cannot possibly do that," we must first recognize the pattern. Next, we need to create a pattern interruption. The interruption must be strong enough to grab your attention away from the ingrained thought, so that you have time to cancel and replace it with a positive and helpful statement.

An interruption could be as simple as saying aloud, "Stop," when you catch your internal conversation saying a negative or limiting statement. The interruption that has worked best for me is wearing a rubber band around my wrist, which I gently snap when I catch myself thinking or speaking unsupportive statements. The sting is enough to grab my attention and buy me enough time to come up with a contrary statement to replace the original thought. Then I say, "Cancel, cancel. That is not the truth."

Let's look at the individual steps required to move unsupportive thinking to positive, supportive thinking.

Applying the Cancel, Cancel Technique

Here are specific steps to implementing the technique yourself.

1. Every morning place a rubber band loosely around your wrist.

2. Stay conscious of your thoughts, especially when you are doing mundane things that don't take a lot of focus.

3. Notice the limiting, unsupportive, or negative thoughts that come into your mind.

4. Immediately, upon recognizing the thought, snap the rubber band against your wrist.

5. Say aloud, "Cancel, cancel! That is not the truth. The truth is _____."

6. Replace the limiting thought with a positive or more accurate statement. If choosing a statement that is the complete opposite feels like a stretch, choose a statement that is a powerful improvement. For example, replace the thought, "I don't have what it takes to be a top tier salesperson," with, "The truth is, I'm a great salesperson." If this seems too bold, try replacing it with, "The truth is, I have the potential to be a top tier salesperson if I focus and work my plan."

From the top, the process sounds like this:

1. Thought or word: "I don't have what it takes to be a top tier salesperson."

2. Snap – Ouch!

3. "Cancel, cancel! That's not the truth. The truth is that I have the potential and know-how to be a top tier salesperson if I stay focused and continue to work the plan.

Got it? Good!

Technique #5: Worry-Busting

"People become attached to their burdens sometimes more than the burdens are attached to them."
~ *George Bernard Shaw*

Let's get logical about worry. We both know that worry is never logical. That's the point. But did you know that there are two kinds of worry, regular worry and unnecessary worry? In truth, all worry is unnecessary because worry is focused on a future that hasn't yet occurred. There is very little you can do about the future.

Now, I imagine that you want to argue that point with me. Heck, even I want to argue the point with myself. So, here goes.

My argument about worry is this: When I worry about the future, I recognize that I'm trying to control the outcome of events that have not taken shape yet. My position is that there are things I can do now in hopes of preparing for or influencing the outcome of those future events.

The rebuttal to the argument above is this: Yes. If there are things you can do to help prepare for or enhance the outcome of those future events, by all means, do them.

But don't worry about them. Worrying wastes time and energy and does nothing to advance you to your goal.

Let's take another look at worry.

1. Take a moment to reflect on the last thing you worried about. What was it? *In my case, it was about a proposal I sent to a potential client from whom I had not heard back.*

2. What were your concerns about? What were you worrying about, specifically? *I worried that I wouldn't get hired.*

3. Did you do all that you needed to do to prepare for the outcome? *Yes.*

4. Was there a benefit to you worrying about the outcome? (Was it going to change the outcome one way or another?) *No benefit. No influence.*

Worry is always focused on possible negative outcomes, right? On the things we fear will happen or might not happen, and the pain or upset we expect to experience by not having our expectations met. Worry is never about the positive. When was the last time you worried about having things go your way? When did you ever worry about having your expectations exceeded? I bet you said, "Never." Right? That's what I thought.

When we put our attention and psychic energy into worrying, we begin to magnetize the unwanted outcomes to ourselves. It's like saying to God, "Hey God, this is Cheryl. I want you to deliver on all these negative outcomes that I've been concentrating on." I'm pretty sure that is not the message you want to convey to the most powerful entity in the universe.

Many people have a built-in habit of worrying. Some folks my parents age and older have established patterns early on due to the circumstances in which they were raised. My father's family was quite poor when he was a child. He grew up with his three sisters in South Florida during the 1940s. Back then, a family of five was difficult to feed, especially on the salary of a furniture maker. Thinking back on my father's upbringing, it's not surprising to learn that my dad held on to everything. That became painfully evident when my brothers and I were clearing out his home after his passing and found literally truckloads of random paper, metal, and wood. Throughout his life, my dad worried about there not being enough— enough money, enough paper, enough metal brackets and nails, enough table legs and scrap wood—when he needed it. I believe that he adopted a habit of worrying early on, that he never outgrew.

Worry for the sake of worry is a waste of valuable time, energy, and emotion. When we spend time worrying about what may or may not happen, it consumes creative energy that could be channeled toward profitable outcomes. Yet, in many cases, we just can't help ourselves, because we don't have adequate tools for recognizing and interrupting our own patterns.

Over the years, I've known several people who don't show signs of worry. This caused me to be curious, I wanted to know if I could be more like them, so I started asking questions to learn their secrets. One discovery

I made was that how much you worry may have to do with your personality style. Those who have a dominant personality style seem to exhibit fewer outward signs of worry, as compared to those who are cautious thinkers or peacemakers. Cautious thinkers and peacemakers tend to be more skeptical in nature and therefore show signs of worry more often.

I believe that people who don't worry ask several reflective questions. I've taken these questions and turned them into a technique call "The Worry-Busting Technique."

1. Given the situation, what is the worst-case scenario?

2. Is the outcome I'm worried about a real possibility? What's the likelihood of this occurring?

3. What does it mean (what have I made up) about me if the worst-case scenario occurs?

4. Is the meaning I gave it about me true?

    a. If the answer to number 4 is "**No,**" make a conscious effort to recognize that the meaning is fabricated and lives in your imagination. Dwelling on the false meaning will result in you adopting it into your belief system. This can lead to emotional paralysis, causing you to get stuck in worry or fear.

    b. If your answer is "**Yes,**" ask yourself two additional questions.

        I. What action can I take to influence or change the outcome?

        II. Am I willing to take the action I've identified now? If not now, when?

Having the answers to these questions gives you greater control over your circumstances. Each of the questions above provides insight and gives you the power to choose. Your answers to these questions are important when it comes to restoring your personal power and stopping worry. Without these insights, your worry can quickly exhaust your energy and derail your focus. This happened to me when I was planning a public seminar for parents of children with learning differences.

My story started three months before the workshop date. My assistant and I sat down to draft how I would like the workshop to go. As the weeks passed, I became more worried about filling the room with participants. Honestly, I was gripped by the fear that no one would come. I felt that if people didn't come, it meant I was a failure. To add to the concern, I also feared I'd suffer a financial loss of several thousand dollars, wasted time, and embarrassment in front of my co-sponsor. My worst-case scenario played out in my head over and over, all day, every day.

Meanwhile, my logical mind argued that it wasn't a waste no matter how many showed up. Someone would get value from it. My rational brain tried to remind me that even though I spent lots of time and money, anyone who received the brochure and didn't attend would assume they missed out on a cool event. Every positive statement I gave myself did little to waylay my fears. Silently, I felt like a failure even before the event took place.

Had I known these worry-busting questions then, I might have felt differently going into the event.

Let's see how the scenario might have played out had I used the technique.

1. My worst-case scenario was that no one would come to the event. On top of the shame and embarrassment I would feel regarding the failure of the event, it would also cost me approximately $1500.

2. The outcome I predicted of zero attendees was unlikely because I knew I had a sponsor who was sending four people.

3. Having the worst-case scenario occur would mean that I would write a story in my head that said I suck at marketing public seminars and I should quit doing it.

4. By asking myself if statement number 3, is true, I would have to say, "No, it is not true. It is a fabrication of my imagination."

If I had taken the time to honestly walk through the worry-busting technique, I might have realized how much of my worry was in my imagination. Unfortunately, the worry consumed me for months, robbing me of creative energy, enthusiasm, and the ability to be fully present on the day of the seminar. Thinking back on it now, I wish I had discovered this technique back then. These simple questions could have shown me just how far down the rabbit hole I'd gone and would have helped me to find my way out.

When you understand that worry comes from a place of feeling out of control, you can approach worry with simple logic. Using your logical left brain will help you return to a state of being in control. Being in control means that you have choices, which puts you back in control and lessens the emotional overload.

Applying the Worry-Busting Technique

1. What is the worst-case scenario?

2. Is the outcome I'm worried about a real possibility?

3. What does it mean if the worst-case scenario comes true?

4. Is the meaning I gave it true?

    a. If the answer to number 4 was no, recognize that the worry was fabricated and only lives in your imagination.

    b. If the answer was yes, ask two additional questions.

        I. What action can I take to influence or change the outcome?

        II. Am I willing to take the action I've identified at this time? If not, when?

Technique #6: Fear-Busting

"Love is what we are born with.
Fear is what we learned here."
~ Marianne Williamson

The purpose of this technique is to neutralize the areas of our lives where fear is running the show and keeping us stuck.

As I mentioned earlier, I had planned a half-day workshop for parents of children with learning differences, ADD, ADHD, autism, etc. What is important to know here is that I felt a fair amount of fear in committing to this project because of the risk involved. Designing, promoting, and presenting any kind of public workshop is risky, because you never know if you will make a return on your investment of time and money. Without the right number of people signing up and paying, the event would not break even financially. What added to the fear was that I had hosted a similar event a year earlier that had lower than desired attendance, in addition to several other "problematic" issues. So, my anxiety was high going into the event.

In the case of the previous event, I worked tirelessly for months to get the word out to those who were my target attendees. I marketed to various parent groups, pediatric offices, and parent support groups, as well as on Facebook and to churches. Ultimately, I had eighteen participants, far fewer than the number I had dreamt of. To make matters worse, the work it required never seemed to end, even after the workshop was over.

Recalling the energy required to put on the first event, I wasn't sure I wanted to try it again. But something inside was guiding me, pushing me to do it, even though there was a ton of "what if" questions parading through my mind. What if no one comes? What if I work just as hard and don't make enough money to break even? What if they do come and they don't like the content? What if this? What if that?

I tried to ignore all the internal self-sabotaging conversations and set a date for the next workshop. A few minutes after choosing a date, I had a moment of brilliant self-awareness. I realized that what I was experiencing was fear, in all its scary, wicked glory. That was it! I was afraid.

The question I needed to ask myself was, what was I afraid of? It was time for me to get clear on the specific fears that were at work and determine if they were real or fabricated.

To help me discover what I was afraid of, I asked myself two questions: What is it I fear? What concerns do I have regarding presenting this workshop?

These were the answers that showed up:

- It will require a ton of energy up front.

- No one will show up, meaning fewer than ten people.

- Too many people will show up, meaning fifty of more.

- I won't meet their expectations.

- I'll be stressed out every day up until the date.

- I'll feel a sense of desperation, like I did last May.

- I don't want to feel that way.

- Someone will be disappointed in me.

- I'll set an expectation and won't be able to deliver.

- They won't like me.

- I'll lose money on the event.

As I looked over my answers, I realized the truth and fiction of the statements, and made a few agreements with myself. The truth was, it would require some time but not a huge amount. I could plan to cancel if fewer than ten people signed up by three days prior to the event. I could also limit the maximum number of people to a number I'm comfortable with. I could clearly define what I was offering in my marketing materials, so people would know what they were getting. I could choose to not be stressed out and instead make it fun. I could give myself permission to stop when I started feeling stressed.

I also realized that there was no reason for desperation. Unlike the last time, there were no fees that I had to pay, so there was no problem. I told myself that all the worry was due to made up thoughts. There was no reason to believe I wouldn't do a good job, because I've always done a great job when I train or speak. And I needed to remember that people trust me.

After I saw the truth of the situation, I asked myself another question, "What is my heart's desire regarding this event?"

I realized I wanted to...

- be of service to these parents

- help them feel better

- teach them the skills to calm their stressed-out nervous systems

- help them feel more hopeful and positive about their situation

- help them get beyond feeling stuck and start moving again

- help them regain their power

- help them to feel empowered, understood, and supported

- help them to know they are loved

I used the fear-busting technique to identify what was holding me back from being fully engaged in the process and to decide whether it was important enough to stop me from moving forward. Ultimately, I decided that all my concerns were made up, fabricated, baloney. It was just my ego trying to do its job of protecting me once again.

Applying the Fear-Busting Technique

1. Divide a sheet of paper into three columns. Label the left column "Fears and Concerns." Label the middle column "Heart's Desires." Label the third column "The Truth."

2. In the left column, make a list of your fears or concerns regarding a specific topic. Don't concern yourself with whether they make sense or are petty. Don't judge; just list. Write as many as you can, and then try to come up with three more. Be as specific as possible.

3. Use these three questions as prompts to help you get beneath the surface. Keep coming back to these three questions to find additional fears, worries, and concerns.

- What do I fear will happen if I _____?

- What are my concerns regarding _____?

- What am I most concerned about?

4. In the center column write down your heart's desires regarding the topic. What do you hope to accomplish, contribute, or feel?

5. Read each fear from the first column out loud to yourself. Take a couple of moments to reflect on one at a time. Ask yourself, "What's the truth behind this fear or concern?" In the third column, write down what surfaces. Don't judge it; just acknowledge it by writing it down.

6. After you have reviewed your concerns, sit quietly. Ask, "What else might be behind this concern?" Capture in writing any additional thoughts or themes. You may recall a person or event that contributed to building the fears. Jot down those memories. Once the backstories have been noted, use the cancel, cancel technique to neutralize them. Repeat the process for additional fears or concerns. You will wipe out the fear and be ready to move towards your goals.

Fears & Concerns	Heart's Desires	The Truth

Section Three
Shifting the Energy

This section is about exploring the techniques you can use to influence your emotional energy, that is, moving your energy from the lower half of the Emotional Hierarchy Chart—where worry, doubt, frustration, and boredom live—to above the line. Above the line is where optimism, enthusiasm, passion, and joy reside. When you can shift your energy at will, you will have become an emotional master. Let's get started!

Technique # 7: Smudging – Cleansing Unwanted Negative Energy

"Derived from the Greek word 'em' (in) and 'pathos' (feeling), the term 'empath' refers to a person who is able to 'feel into' the feelings of others."
~ *Mateo Sol,* Awakened Empath: The Ultimate Guide to Emotional, Psychological, and Spiritual Healing

D o you ever feel a little bit off? You know, when you feel like you are not at your brightest and best. Or that feeling you get when you leave a meeting or a networking event, and you feel kind of icky.

Every time we interact with another human being, we encounter their energy. We don't even have to have a conversation with them. Think about it. Have you ever gotten on an elevator that you couldn't wait to leave, because the energy of the people on it made you uncomfortable? That's the kind of energy I'm talking about.

Before my husband Marvin and I had children, we held bi-monthly discussion groups. We would invite a few deep-thinker-type friends to our house for an evening of conversation. We explored subjects like the power of positive thinking, spirituality, parallel universes, and time travel. During one of those meetings we focused on the topic of angels. It was at that meeting that one of the regular participants brought a friend.

The friend had heard about our group and was interested in participating. Throughout the discussion, the friend seemed cordial and participated in the conversation. On the surface, she seemed nice enough. Nothing she did gave us reason to be concerned. It was after the meeting that we noticed a weird energy in the house—as if a residue was left behind. Like when a heavy smoker enters a room, sometimes there is a musty smoke odor that remains when they leave.

Let me be clear here. The residue wasn't a smell. It was an energy. An energy we had never before felt following the discussion group. (As I shared with you earlier, I tend to be highly sensitive to the energy of people, places, and things. I can sense if the energy is positive, neutral, or negative.)

Initially, when I felt the strange energy, I thought I was being over-reactive, so I kept my thoughts to myself and didn't even share them with Marvin. When the energy got weird the second time she attended, I could no longer keep my mouth shut. That evening after everyone left, I approached Marvin to see if he noticed anything. He said, "As a matter of fact, I did. It was like there was a heavy wet blanket over the room." I responded by saying, "Yes, and that blanket was oppressive and sucked the energy out of the room." Up until the new person joined us, the energy of the group had been light and pleasant. But this energy felt sinister. As Marvin and I talked about it, we realized that the only new element to the group was the woman.

As we analyzed the events of the evening, we checked to see if we had invited negativity into our home with our discussion topic. We agreed that we had not. The conversation that evening was light and very positive. Not knowing the source or purpose of the energy, we decided to smudge the house with sage.

Smudging is a process that Native Americans used to cleanse the energy of an individual. Because other people's energy can stick to you, smudging is one way to release it from your body. It is a simple process, requiring dried sage rolled into a tight bundle. You light the sage with a lighter or match. Once it catches, you blow it out, allowing it to smoke. Native Americans used an eagle or hawk feather to fan the smoke over an individual or throughout a room, making sure to direct the smoke in every direction, high and low. This process wards off and neutralizes negative energy and evil spirits.

I immediately went to retrieve our sage bundle to begin the process. We smudged the entire downstairs and kitchen areas. We smudged the front porch and upstairs too, just to be on the safe side. We wanted to make sure that every ounce of negativity was neutralized. And it worked! We both felt an immediate lift of the negative energy. Within ten minutes the energy of our happy home had returned.

Applying the Smudging Technique

1. Collect, dry, and roll your sage into a bundle or purchase a premade sage stick.

2. Light the end of the sage stick on fire. It will be slow to burn. Blow it out after it has caught fire, leaving it smoking.

3. Fan the smoke to all corners of the room walking in a counter-clockwise direction around the room.

4. Fan the smoke up toward the ceiling, and then down toward the floor.

5. Fan the smoke on individuals who may have negative energy stuck to them.

6. Hold the intention in your mind that you are rejecting all the negative energy and evil from the room. Repeat the intention out loud if you feel you need to.

7. Make a complete circle around the room.

8. Close by saying, "I invite only love and light that has never been reprogrammed by the dark to return to this room."

9. Put the sage stick out by grinding it into an ashtray, making sure that all embers are out. Go on about your business, free from negative energy.

Technique #8: The Centering Technique

"Your true power does not come from your physical action, but from your vibrational alignment."
~ Abraham

A wkward and even contrary energy of another can significantly influence how we feel, so much so that it can also throw off our body's natural energy balance. Spending too much time with people or environments that are not a match for you can cause an imbalance in your energy field. The good news is there is a technique to bring you back into balance; it's called "The Centering Technique." When I use this technique, it feels like I've restored positive energy and natural balance to my system.

Applying the Centering Technique

1. Place your fingertips on your chest, about three inches below your collarbone and in alignment with the nipple (where the large black dots are on the diagram). You will notice a slight indentation in the chest muscles in this location. We call this area the sore spot, because it is usually a tender spot.

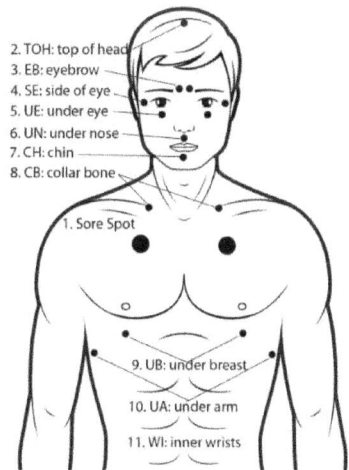

2. TOH: top of head
3. EB: eyebrow
4. SE: side of eye
5. UE: under eye
6. UN: under nose
7. CH: chin
8. CB: collar bone
1. Sore Spot
9. UB: under breast
10. UA: under arm
11. WI: inner wrists

2. Rub this spot using a circular motion in either direction.

3. While continuing to rub circles on the sore spot, repeat the following statement three times. "Even though my polarities may be reversed, I ask them to come into perfect alignment and balance now."

4. With your fingertips, gently tap the top of your head while saying, "I ask my polarities to become perfectly aligned and balanced now."

5. Using two fingers, tap on the inner eyebrow five to seven times, while repeating the phrase, "I ask my polarities to become perfectly aligned and balanced now."

6. Next, with two fingers, gently tap on the outside of the eye on the occipital bone and repeat the phrase again.

7. Tap under the eye and repeat the phrase.

8. Tap under the nose and repeat the phrase.

9. Tap on the chin indent just below the bottom lip and repeat the phrase.

10. Tap on the collarbone and repeat the phrase.

11. Tap under the breast muscle (men) or bra-line (women).

12. Tap under the arm.

13. Tap the inner wrists together.

14. Take two deep breaths.

Notice the subtle energy shifts within your body. You may feel a little light-headed, as I often do. If you don't feel anything, don't worry; you are doing it right.

Technique # 9: Intention Setting

"When you have clarity of intention, the Universe conspires with you to make it happen."
~ Fabienne Fredrickson

When my children were in primary school, it felt like my life was in a constant state of gray. There was no color to my days. Each day looked like the one before. My work day routine was tedious. Day after day was pretty much the same—boring and uneventful. Not only did each day feel like the color gray, so did my emotional state. I needed some color and I needed it quick!

I shared my colorless existence with a friend, Jennifer Orhman. Jen suggested that I use a technique called daily intention setting. She suggested that I create an intention at the beginning of each day. The intention would outline what I wanted to feel that day. At the end of the day, I was to notice the number of times I felt the desired feeling. This was an entirely new concept. I had heard of setting intentions, but I always regarded them as things to accomplish, tasks or goals. Thinking of them in terms of how I wanted to feel was a crazy idea.

The very next day I tried Jen's technique. My intention was to feel light and happy. That evening, as I lay in bed, I reviewed the day, taking a mental inventory of what I felt during that day. I recalled all the times I felt light or happy during the day. I immediately started to smile. I could see several times during the day when I had felt light and happy. I was amazed at how well this intention setting thing worked, so I tried again the next day. And, yes, it worked again!

The purpose of setting a daily intention is to attract positive events into your experiences. These seemingly elusive, yet desirable experiences are not hard to come by when you use this technique. You can decide at any point of the day to set an intention. You might set an intention for how you would like a conversation to go. You might set an intention for how you would like to feel during a meeting or a networking event. Let's say you are required to attend a company training session that you have no interest in. You could set an intention for what you would like to experience and feel while you are in the training. Maybe you would like to experience having fun, enjoying the company of others, or learning something new you can immediately use. Imagine the possibilities if you were on the lookout for certain kinds of experiences.

When I tried setting an intention during an international conference, I was overwhelmed by the cool people I met each day. All were warm and friendly and shared specific business and marketing insights that later helped my business. The results can be surprising when you are intentional about what you want to experience and feel.

Applying the Daily Intention Setting Technique

1. Begin by getting centered. Use the centering technique or just take several of deep cleansing breaths before you begin.

2. Identify how you would like to feel today. Do you want to feel light, joyful, energetic, peaceful, relaxed, calm, centered, confident, motivated, loving, or maybe even sexy?

3. Add your desired descriptors or feelings to the following phrase. "Today, I consciously choose to feel _____ throughout my day. Spirit, please bring me opportunities to experience these chosen feelings and the awareness to recognize them when they are present. Namaste."

4. At the end of the day, as you lie in bed, review the day's events and interactions. Notice when and how often you felt your desired feeling. What were you doing when you felt it? Who were you with? Did your feelings have a color associated with them? I bet it wasn't gray.

By setting intentions you are placing an order with the Universal Power, God, who makes all things possible. Making a request through an intention statement activates the energy that magnetizes similar energies to you. Your request says, "Hey, this is the kind of energy I want to experience. Bring me experiences of that kind of energy." If you intend to feel loved today, then you will likely encounter opportunities to be loving. As a result, you will feel loved.

Have fun with this technique. Make different requests every other day to see what results you get. Pay attention to your thoughts. Sometimes they want to challenge the power of this technique, which will delay the delivery of your request. Stay positive and optimistic.

Technique #10: Pre-Paving the Way

"What we see depends mainly on what we look for."
~ John Lubbock, 1ˢᵗ Baron Avebury

For Jill, a new outside sales representative at a printing company, the idea of making sales calls pushed her feelings of apprehension to an all-time high. Up until recently, Jill's role had been one of "order taker" rather than "salesperson." Her boss's expectations were high—thirty calls per week, with at least ten follow-up calls from the week prior. That meant that she had to visit thirty potential customers at their place of business each week and phone the top ten prospects from the week before. Not only was she overwhelmed by the number of contacts she had to make, but by the thought of what would undoubtedly happen when she reached those prospects.

She had heard from others that she should be ready for people to be downright ugly and abusive toward her when she called on them. She worried that the people she was to contact would be impolite, even nasty to her. It didn't matter that she had never personally experienced that kind of treatment. She was feeling anxious at even the possibility of it happening.

The more she thought about what could happen, the more she was reluctant to leave the print shop. Each time she looked down at the list of people she was to call on, she felt tension building in her chest. That tension then moved down to her stomach. It felt like a rope tightening in her belly, making it hard for her to breathe. When the tension started to come on, she tried to comfort herself by saying, "This is part of the job. If they say no, it's no big deal. It's not about me." "It's no big deal and it's not about me," became her mantra. She repeated the mantra over to herself, but it did little to squelch her stress and nervousness. She tried deep breathing, because someone told her it was a good way to calm her nerves, but that didn't seem to help either.

Without realizing it, Jill kept repeating the worst-case scenarios over in her head. As a result, she adopted a story—someone else's story—as her own. She painted a picture of how she thought the sales calls might go. The story she created was based on ill-fated stories of another's experiences and their discomfort with making sales calls. From her observations of others, she created projections of how she expected the story to go for her. Of course, none of it was true, since she hadn't yet left the office.

Each of us writes our own story projecting how we think things will play out. The sad part is that as you imagine your story, you are also crafting the outcome. The more you plan for a negative outcome, the more likely you are to create that same result. Universal law states, "What you expect to see, you will receive." If you expect to be treated poorly, you will likely be treated in the manner you were expecting. The same is true in the reverse; expect to be treated well and you will be.

So, what if you were to draft the story with a different ending? An ending that you would prefer.

One of the ways that I've found to reduce my feelings of stress and anxiety is to use a technique called "Pre-Paving the Way." Think of pre-paving as putting down a foundation, laying the asphalt before you drive on the road. Pre-paving is writing the story before it has begun. It is also writing all the way through, from introduction to conclusion. You wouldn't want the asphalt to run out soon after you entered the freeway. Wouldn't you want it to run all the way to your destination? So, you craft the story of what you want to have happen, from beginning to end, instead of allowing your anxious mind to run willy-nilly, creating a fearful tale.

Quite often, our minds will dream up the worst-case scenario to prepare us for and protect us from upset or perceived danger. At the most basic level, our brains are preprogramed for survival. The limbic system of the brain, also known as the reptilian brain, located in the back and base of the skull, is always on the lookout for danger. We refer to the limbic system's response to danger as the *fight or flight response*. When the limbic brain perceives a threat, it goes into hyper-vigilant mode, releasing hormones and endorphins that cause anxiety. These hormones and endorphins prepare us for action—they prepare us to fight, take flight, or freeze. (By the way, they often cause us to prepare for danger even when there is no actual threat.) In Jill's cold-calling experience, her response was to freeze. She was so frozen in place that she could not seem to get out of the office. Even with all the positive self-talk in the world, she couldn't muster the strength to get started. Until…until she pre-paved the way.

During one of Jill's private coaching sessions, we talked about her inability to get started. I asked her to describe the thoughts and images that came to mind right before she was to leave the office to call on someone. I said, "Tell me the story of how it would happen."

Without hesitation she said, "I just know the person I'm about to go see is going to give me a hard time. I imagine it to be a man. And he'll say that he doesn't have time for me and tell me to go f-off or something." I could clearly see why Jill was hesitant to make calls on people with that story running in her head. No wonder her anxiety was so high and she was frozen in place in the safety of the office.

After I acknowledged her and her story, I suggested the possibility that there might be an alternative story she hadn't thought of. She leaned her head to one side and asked, "What could that be?"

"Would you be willing to try on a different story?" I asked. She said she would. So I encouraged her to imagine calling on someone and the visit going perfectly. Just the way she would like it to, as if she were the script writer and director of a movie. How would the scene play out? I asked her to describe it to me using a lot of detail. How would the characters respond to one another? What would they say? How would they feel? How would the visit end?

As Jill started to describe the details of the perfect sales call, she closed her eyes. It was as if she was there, in the moment of it. I questioned, "Can you see it happening the way you are describing it?" She responded, "Yes," and continued. "I see myself walking into the prospect's office and asking to speak to him. The receptionist is friendly and offers me a cup of coffee. I say, 'No, thank you.' Without hesitation she lets the prospect know I am there and he comes right out to see me. He's warm and friendly as he offers his hand to shake mine. I introduce myself and tell him why I'm there. I explain that we specialize in commercial printing, and we are usually less expensive than other shops in the area. We continue talking and I learn that he had been thinking of doing a direct mail campaign for his company. He asks me if I would be willing to put together a quote. I smile and tell him, 'Quotes are what I do best.' As we finish our conversation, I hand him my business card. He gives me his. I promise to get back to him within twenty-four hours with a quote. I thank him for his time, and he lets me know it was a pleasure meeting me. I leave the business feeling proud and excited that I will soon have a client of my own."

As Jill finished her description, I noticed a smile come across her face. I asked her how she is feeling about making the sales call now? She responded, "I feel great. I know I can do this."

Two weeks later at our next session, I checked in with Jill to see how the sales calls had been going. She reported that just that week she had made twenty calls and had written eight quotes. She said that she was feeling pretty proud of herself and that it was hard to believe she had ever been afraid to call on people.

Pre-paving the way with the story you want to experience increases your chances of living that experience by 65 percent. What limiting story have you been telling yourself? Are you ready to shift that story from negative to positive? Here's how.

Applying the Pre-Paving the Way Technique

1. Recognize what your anxiety or fear is about.

2. Briefly outline the story that keeps you from moving forward.

3. Then, close your eyes and re-imagine your situation with a new storyline. Revise the story from an ideal perspective. If everything were to happen perfectly, what would it look like? Describe what you would say. What would be the ideal response from others in the story? Describe how you would feel. Be careful not to let your biases about those people influence your new story. Don't forget to describe the most positive outcome you can dream up.

4. Review the new preferred story. Imagine it going exactly as you scripted it.

5. Then, act. Go do what you need to do, with the pre-paved story as your expectation and see what happens.

6. Afterwards, take a few minutes to compare the actual events to your pre-paved preferred story. Notice the similarities and differences. Did the actual events go as you described them? Were there any hidden surprises? Could you have prepared any better? Did the interaction turn out better than you expected?

Technique #11: Shift Your Energy Through Quality Questions

"The quality of your life is determined by the quality of the questions you ask yourself."
~ *Kevin McDonald, Canadian performance coach*

Think about it—do you ever ask yourself questions? Questions like: Why does this always happen to me? Why can't I catch a break like other people? Why am I so unlucky in relationships? Why is running a business, getting new clients, and making money so easy for some but not me? Why do I continue to struggle?

What do all these questions have in common? Right, the word *why*. But that's not the answer I'm looking for. Look more closely.

Here's a hint, what are the questions focused on? They are focused on what you don't have or what is not working in your life. Do you think there might be a correlation between what you focus on and what you get? You betcha!

Let's go back to Kevin's statement, "The quality of your life is determined by the quality of the questions you ask yourself." If you're asking questions that focus on *what's missing* or how you are not meeting your own expectations, then circumstances are not likely to improve. However, if you shift your focus and your questions from what's not right to how you can take personal responsibility, the results will amaze you.

Try shifting your focus and your questions by asking *how* and *what* questions. For example:

- What actions have I taken that led me to this reoccurring result?

- What can I do to set up my day to have more ease and flow?

- What actions can I take that will lead me to quality people with values like mine?

- What in my environment needs to be cleaned up or cleared out for me to experience greater calmness in my life?

- How can I attract clients that I would really enjoy working with?

- How can I create routines that make my business easier to run?

- What can I do to attract better, healthier relationships?

- How can I create more space and time so that I can have more freedom?

- What actions can I take to improve my relationships at work?

- What systems can I put into place to keep me from reaching burnout?

By changing the focus of your questions, you elevate the quality of the answers you receive. Let's say your question was, "**Why do I always get stuck with these crummy jobs?**" In this scenario, you are blaming someone else for assigning you the crappy job. Blaming someone else disempowers you. It's like saying that you have no control over your life.

Notice what happens to your energy when you shift the focus and ask this question instead: "**What action do I need to take to get the fun and interesting jobs?**"

Can you feel the shift in your energy when you ask this question versus the previous one? Positioning the question in the form of "what action can I take" is empowering, motivating, activating, and encouraging. The best time to use this technique is when you feel stuck or taken advantage of or when you start to blame others for your circumstances. Practicing this technique shifts your energy and activates your personal power. When you are in a position of 100 percent responsibility, you become incredibly powerful.

Applying Quality Questions

1. Using the word "why" at the beginning of each question, make a list of the top ten areas in your life that are not going as you would prefer. For example: Why can't I get a better job? Why aren't good things happening for me? Why do I feel bad? Why doesn't my boss see what I am doing and promote me? Why do so many other people get what they want, and I don't?

2. Focusing on only one question at a time, rewrite the question. This time, shift the focus to be actionable by starting the question with one of the following words: "what" or "how." For example: How can I get a better job? What can I change in me to have good things happen for me? What do I need to do to prepare for a promotion?

3. Review your list of actionable questions and choose one to act on. You don't have to know the steps you will take. Leave it to your creative right brain to determine your inspired next steps. It will provide you with the most appropriate actions.

4. To identify your next inspired steps, allow your mind to dwell on the question without pushing it. Repeat the question in your head. Ideas may not surface immediately. Just keep dwelling on the question. When ideas or suggestions surface, capture them. Avoid judging them as good, bad, or unhelpful. The longer you dwell on the question, the richer the ideas will be.

5. Follow the same process for the other questions. Ultimately, you will have enough ideas to build a plan of action to achieve what you desire. Asking "what" and "how" questions empowers you to take charge of your circumstances.

Cheryl C Jones

Technique #12: Break Free with the Emotional Freedom Technique

"You can't get to your next best self by clinging to who you were yesterday."
~ *Robin Sharma*

Whether your age is nine or ninety-nine, sometime during your life you've experienced trauma. As a child, your trauma may have been due to a fall off your bike. As a more mature person, one of your traumas may have included a breakup or losing your partner.

Trauma can be described as events—real or imagined—that trigger strong emotional reactions. Trauma can also be physical or psychological, or a combination of both. One such situation occurred to me at the age of twenty-four.

Freshly graduated from college and two months into my first corporate job, I purchased my dream car—a late model Mercury Cougar in metallic midnight blue with beige interior. It was a sweet ride. One morning on my way to work through Houston freeway traffic, I was rear-ended by a massive pick-up truck with a huge steel grill on the front. The cause of the accident was the driver's last-minute decision to cross three lanes of traffic to reach the exit. I saw the driver changing lanes and slowed down to avoid her. That's when it happened, bam! The heavy-duty pickup truck rear-ended my car, sending me sailing 100 feet down the freeway before I could bring it to a stop. It also set off a chain reaction that resulted in a five-car pileup.

As we all waited for the police to arrive, I stood stunned and in shock, leaning against the center barricade as traffic continued to fly by. I would later realize that the accident resulted in not only a bad case of whiplash but some psychological trauma as well. I began to fear driving in Houston. For a year after the accident, I took surface roads to and from work to avoid driving on the freeway. And anytime I heard screeching tires on pavement, my body would tense up, automatically bracing for impact. The fear and anxiety had become anchored in my body due to the accident.

In addition, I was also harboring guilt, embarrassment, and shame. You see, about a minute or so before the crash, I looked in my rearview mirror and saw the truck behind me with its huge front bumper. Immediately, a thought came rushing through my awareness. (It turned out to be a premonition.) That thought was a cross between a picture and a feeling, but the message was clear—I was about to get hit by that truck.

(Let's pause here for a second and allow me to let you in on a little-known secret.) Throughout my childhood and into my twenties, I often had premonitions of events that would come true. It happened so frequently that it kind of freaked me out.

Back to the story of guilt, embarrassment, and shame. At some level, I felt responsible for the accident. I told myself, because I had received the message regarding the accident, I should have been able to change the outcome. That's why I felt guilty. I felt embarrassed because I thought I should have known to do something differently—been a better driver or avoided the accident somehow. And I felt shame because I allowed the accident to happen.

Now to you, this logic may sound absurd. I agree! It isn't logical. But that is how emotions sometimes run. My logical mind was not processing. My thoughts had run amuck, causing my emotions to heighten. My logical mind wasn't doing the processing. Instead, my limbic system—the fight, flight, or freeze system—had taken over.

Earlier, I mentioned that trauma can also be imagined. Traumatic events don't have to be real or even first-hand experiences to leave a lasting emotional impression.

When our children were young, we had a babysitter named Audrey. Since she babysat every Monday night, we got to know Audrey quite well. One night, as she was about to leave, she mentioned that she wasn't in a big hurry to get home. When we asked her why, she said that she had a hard time getting to sleep. Even though she was a junior in high school, and lived with her parents and two brothers, she was afraid to go to sleep at night. Upon further questioning, we learned that about eight months earlier she had watched a movie in which the killer lurked under the bed while the woman slept. In the scene that followed, the killer's hand sprang up through the mattress to grab the woman. Audrey said that every night before bed, she would routinely check under her bed before climbing in. Even though there was never anything there, she still couldn't sleep for fear the movie scene would materialize in her room. Audrey experienced trauma from an imagined event.

Because my husband, Marvin, and I adored Audrey, we hated to see her living with such intense fear, so we offered her help using The Emotional Freedom Technique. Both of us had been trained in the method, also known as EFT, which involves using your fingertips to tap on ten meridian points of the body to achieve "a neutral emotional state." Often when you experience an intense fear or trauma, your amygdala (the fight or flight area of the brain) is triggered, and your body is flooded with cortisol—the stress hormone. Cortisol is what prepares you to fight or take flight. Audrey's amygdala was triggered every night as she climbed into bed by the memory of the movie; this sent her into a state of fight or flight, or in her case, freeze.

Studies have shown that by stimulating the meridians within your body, you can reduce and even eliminate the stress response, restoring the body to a balanced state. When a disturbance has been neutralized or released, the body's energy flow can return to its natural state, and the person will feel the negative emotions fade away. That is just what happened for Audrey.

Before she left our house that evening, we asked her if she would like to get rid of her fear. She replied, "Yes! Absolutely."

Marvin proceeded to ask her a couple more questions so that he could identify the specific triggers that resonated with her, and then began the tapping process. The entire process took about four minutes. When it was complete, Marvin asked her how she felt. She said the she felt very relaxed. The next Monday night she returned to babysit again. We could not wait to hear how she had slept over the last week. Audrey reported that she had totally forgotten about the problem, and she had slept soundly every night since the previous Monday. The trauma of the movie was now ancient history.

Applying the Emotional Freedom Technique (EFT)

Chinese medicine practitioners use needles placed in specific locations on the body to restore the natural flow of Chi, the life-force energy of the body. Traumatic experiences, strong beliefs, and negative emotions block the flow of Chi. Practitioners believe that when the Chi is flowing freely and correctly along the natural pathways, it restores energy and provides optimum health to the individual. EFT uses the same meridian system to restore the flow of energy that has been blocked by trauma, emotional hurts, and false beliefs. It also works on physical pain. The difference between acupuncture and EFT is that EFT uses light fingertip tapping on the meridians instead of needles to get a similar result. When EFT clears energy blocks, it allows the Chi to return to its natural flow, improving health and happiness.

The good news is that EFT is a technique that you can use anytime, anywhere, to neutralize negative emotions and physical pain. It's safe, simple, painless, and most of all, it is effective. By gently tapping on ten points on your face and upper torso, you can deactivate emotional trauma, release unwanted negative emotions, and neutralize physical pain. Emotions such as fear, sadness, shock, anger, hurt, and shame are just a few of the emotions that can be released using this unique technique. Physical pain like headaches, muscle aches, migraines, and acid reflux can also be reduced or eliminated. Further, it has been used to resolve psychological issues of low self-esteem, unworthiness, and perfectionism.

From personal experience, I can tell you that using this technique has changed my life. I don't want to sound melodramatic, but it is the truth. EFT has helped me neutralize feelings of hurt, betrayal, sadness, anger, fear, and abandonment. It has allowed me to reclaim joy, happiness, and passion. EFT is a powerful tool to have in your self-help arsenal.

Five Steps to Emotional Freedom

There are five simple steps to get started. You don't have to be an expert to start getting relief.

1. Identify the Issue

This may seem like an obvious step; however, many times it is not easy to isolate the real issue. To gain relief from an unwanted emotion or pain, you must first identify what it is you want to be rid of. You are looking for the issue that is most bothersome to you. The thing that made you mad, hurt your feelings, or has caused you physical pain. It is usually not a person, but the *feeling* that we are trying to change. Therefore, if you are feeling lonely or sad, or you have a headache—these are the things you would like changed, not the *person* who left without saying goodbye or who said something that hurt your feelings. For physical pain, you might focus on sinus pressure, a headache, or menstrual cramps with a goal of relieving the physical discomfort. Once you've identified the "focus" you are ready to get down to the business of tapping.

2. Rate the Intensity Level

To assist you in determining your success with tapping, it's important to rate the level of intensity. When you think of the emotional or physical intensity, how strong is it? Using a scale of 0 to 10, determine the intensity of the emotion or pain. A rating of 0 means the item is "neutral" or is no longer causing discomfort. An intensity rating of 10 means that the intensity is as high as it could be.

To determine your intensity rating, check in with your body, focus on the emotion or pain. Ask yourself, "How strong is this emotion (or pain)?" See what number comes to mind. The first number that pops into your head is usually the right number.

3. The Setup Phrase and The Karate Chop Point

The setup phrase is a statement used to start each round of tapping. By constructing a simple phrase that accurately reflects the issue, we let our body know what to focus on. State the setup phrase three times, while continuously tapping on the side of the hand with the fingertips of the other hand—we call this the karate chop point.

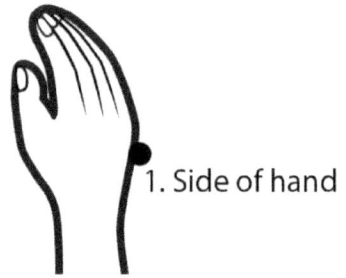

1. Side of hand

The phrase starts with, "Even though…." This lets the body know that you acknowledge the issue and own it as your own. The second part of the setup phrase announces to your system that you love and accept yourself despite having the issue. This statement separates "you" from the problem itself. So, the phrase looks like this:

Even though I'm feeling _____, I deeply and completely love and accept myself.

Here's an example of a setup phrase for speaking in public:

Even though I'm terrified to speak in front of a large audience, I deeply and completely love and accept myself. (Repeat two more times.)

Not all issues fit neatly into the "Even though…" phraseology. So, sometimes it makes sense to change the phrase to accommodate a specific issue. For example, the issue might be the fear of being taken advantage of. You could phrase it like this:

Even though I have a preoccupation with being taken advantage of, I love and accept myself anyway.

An Important Note

It's probably obvious that I have chosen to highlight the negative emotions. This is because the negative emotions are what create the disruption in the energy flow. Disruptions are responsible for both physical and emotional difficulties and have been linked to chronic stress, anxiety, body aches and pains, acne, fear, migraines, etc. Tapping clears the disruption, allowing the energy to return to its natural flow.

4. The Tapping Sequence

The sequence of tapping points activates fourteen energy meridians running through the body. Simply tap five to seven times on each of the locations as you speak openly, describing the issue. Once you've completed tapping on all points, take two deep breaths. Be sure to exhale completely.

The tapping points are listed in order as they occur on the body, with the exception of the karate chop point (KC) and the top of the head (TOH). The karate chop point is the first location and it is used with the setup phrase, "Even though…, I deeply and completely love and accept myself." The top of the head is the last location to tap while saying the reminder phrases.

5. Reminder Phrases

Reminder phrases are statements intended to keep you focused by describing the issue along with its associated aspects and details. They are what you say as you tap through the points, starting with the eyebrow and ending with the top of the head. For example, let's go through a tapping sequence using the number one fear of 90 percent of the population— speaking in front of a live audience. The whole tapping sequence might read as shown below. I've included the tapping points just in case you wanted to try it out yourself.

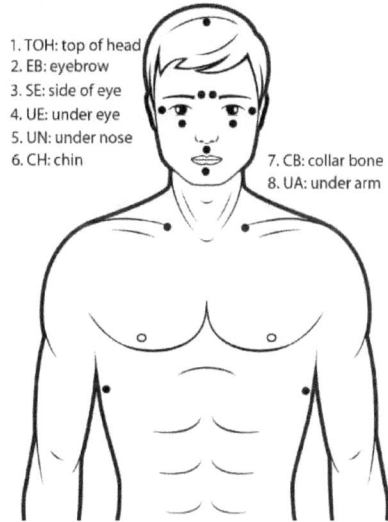

1. TOH: top of head
2. EB: eyebrow
3. SE: side of eye
4. UE: under eye
5. UN: under nose
6. CH: chin
7. CB: collar bone
8. UA: under arm

Reminder Phrases Example

(EB) I have a fear of speaking in front of groups.

(SE) It is so scary. I'm afraid I'll mess up.

(UE) I'm so afraid that the audience will laugh at me or make fun of me.

(UN) I'll feel humiliated if that happens.

(CH) I just know that I will forget my words or my place, and that would be awful.

(CB) I'm so nervous. I know I can't do it.

(UA) I'll mess up and then everyone will remind me of how bad I was at speaking.

(TOH) I'm so afraid that I will embarrass myself.

Take two deep breaths, in and out.

6. Rate the Intensity Again

After you have finished tapping, check in with your body again to rate the level of intensity. Is your rating the same? Different? Be sure to use the same scale you used beforehand of 0 to 10. What did you notice?

If you find that your intensity for an issue has dropped to zero, then you are all done. However, if you find that the intensity has dropped, but not to zero, perform another round of tapping starting at the inner eyebrow point. You can skip the karate chop point and setup phrase. During this round, try to get more specific with your descriptors. In fact, I want you to exaggerate them. Blow them out of proportion. Exaggerations can act as an energetic kick in the pants to help move stuck energy.

To learn more about the Emotional Freedom Technique, visit www.emofree.com. If you would like to see a video on the subject, visit https://tinyurl.com/y8rc9jl3. Or go to YouTube.com and search for "EFT Introduction" to find the video by Gary Craig.

To help you get started with EFT, I have written a couple of tapping scripts that you can practice with. There are eighteen additional scripts in the appendix. If the words in the scripts don't match your exact feelings or experience, feel free to change the language to better meet your needs.

Emotional Freedom Technique
Sample Scripts

Anxiety Due to an Expected Reaction of Someone Else

Setup Phrases

(KC) Even though I'm afraid David will become angry when I tell him that he is fired, I deeply and completely love and accept myself. (Repeat three times, as shown here.)

(KC) Even though I'm afraid David will become angry when I tell him that he is fired, I deeply and completely love and accept myself.

(KC) Even though I'm afraid David will become angry when I tell him that he is fired, I deeply and completely love and accept myself.

Reminder Phrases

(EB) I know that he depends on this job, but he keeps getting into arguments.

(SE) I'm afraid he'll be mad. I'm afraid of his anger.

(UE) I'm afraid that he will take his anger out on me.

(UN) What will I do if he decides to blow up?

(CH) I'm so afraid that he will get violent.

(CB) He frightens me when he gets angry.

(UA) I don't handle it well when other people are angry with me.

(TOH) I'm so afraid of his uncontrollable anger.

(TOH) I'm so afraid that he'll lose control. I hate it when he gets angry.

Take two deep breaths, in and out.

Confidence and Self-Worth

When you've faced a major emotional setback or a major disappointment, like getting fired from your job or being rejected in a love relationship, it can shake your self-confidence and sense of self-worth. Here's a tapping script to help restore confidence.

Setup Phrases

(KC) Even though my confidence and self-worth are not as strong as they used to be, I love and accept myself just the way I am.

(KC) Even though I feel like I'm not the person I once was—confident, strong, capable of just about anything—I deeply and completely love and accept myself.

(KC) Even though I don't feel that I'm the person I used to be—that strong, confident, can-do person—I love and accept myself.

Reminder Phrases

(EB) I'm not the person I used to be. I used to be confident and self-assured. Today, I don't feel as confident as I once did.

(SE) I know I've made some poor decisions in the past. Those decisions have caused me to feel less confident.

(UE) I doubt my value and worth.

(UN) I don't like this lack of confidence I am feeling, this lack of self-worth.

(CH) I continue to feel doubt and unworthy. I hate these feelings.

(CB) My self-doubt makes me question my every decision and move.

(UA) I can't trust myself. I doubt myself.

(TOH) I keep feeling self-doubt and unworthy. I don't feel confident. It's time for me to reclaim my confidence and self-worth.

Take two deep breaths, in and out.

Procrastination – Getting Started on a Project

At some point, everyone is faced with procrastination. The activities that are not immediately rewarding, like paying bills, cleaning the fish tank, completing homework, or going to the dentist, tend to get pushed to the end of the list. Here's a way to take charge of procrastination.

Setup Phrase

(KC) Even though I recognize that I am procrastinating about getting this project (name the topic or project) started (or completed), I deeply and completely love and accept myself.

(KC) Even though I can't seem to get myself going (or take action) on this project, I deeply and completely love and accept myself anyway.

(KC) Even though I can tell that I'm dragging my feet on this project and I don't know why, I deeply and completely love and accept myself anyway.

Reminder Phrases

(EB) Yes, I know I'm procrastinating. I can see that I'm not getting anything done.

(SE) I don't know what's wrong. I can't seem to get motivated.

(UE) I'm stuck in a pattern of inaction, indecision, and procrastination.

(UN) This pattern of putting-off, delay, and avoidance is getting me nowhere.

(CH) I feel so frustrated that I can't get going. I'm stalled, stuck, and at a standstill.

(CB) I keep stalling, hoping I'll feel motivated to do what I need to do. I wish I could just push through it. But there's no motivation.

(UA) I just can't seem to get moving. This feeling, like I'm being held up, held back, stopped, is annoying.

(TOH) I recognize that I'm procrastinating. I'm ready to move past it. Take two deep breaths, in and out

Your Future Happiness is Up to You

Most stressed-out adults I meet today believe two things to be true: 1) They can't control how they feel, 2) Other people have the power to make them feel a certain way. Both statements are false. These false truths have led us to believe that we have little or no control over ourselves. For centuries, this bogus tale has permeated our society, when in actuality, each of us has the power to change our thoughts and feelings, if we choose to do so.

This book is only the beginning. The beginning of your self-made transformation. As you continue to free yourself from patterns of negativity and master the thoughts and emotions that have undermined your confidence and caused self-doubt, you will begin to experience greater happiness and positivity. You'll feel more confident, content, motivated, energized, and yes, peaceful. This is the first step toward feeling inspired, creative, and passionate regarding your work, your relationships, and your life.

This book is intended to be a resource to guide you become a master of your emotions. I hope by reading it, you have found several applications to ease your pain, help you regain your personal power, and restore your self-confidence. When you become a master of your emotions, you return the authority to where it belongs — placing it squarely in your hands. You now have the magical power to destroy the false beliefs that have held your emotions captive for far too long. You now have the knowledge and expertise to change, not only your life, but the world around you. Because when you change the way you interpret the world, the world around you can't help but change too.

I wish you much happiness and joy.

Cheryl

If I can be of further assistance or if after using these techniques you would like to share your results, please feel free to reach out to me via email, at: Cheryl@SimplyTheBestResults.com.

Helpful Resources

The resources listed below are books, websites, and videos that I have found helpful. I hope you will, too.

Books

You Can Heal Your Life, by Louise Hay

Power VS. Force: The Hidden Determinants of Human Behavior, by David R. Hawkins, MD, PhD

Molecules of Emotion: The Science Behind Mind-Body Medicine, by Candice B. Pert, PhD

The Biology of Belief: Unleashing the Power of Consciousness, Matter and Miracles, by Bruce Lipton, PhD

The Attractor Factor: 5 Easy Steps for Creating Wealth (or Anything Else) from the Inside Out, by Joe Vitale

Zero Limits: The Secret Hawaiian System for Wealth, Health, Peace, and More, by Joe Vitale

Anything Is Possible, by Joe Vitale

The Energy of Belief: Psychology's Power Tools to Focus Intention and Release Blocking Beliefs, Sheila Sidney Bender, PhD, and Mary T. Sise, LCSW

The Four Agreements, by Don Miguel Ruiz

How to Be Your Own Best Friend, by Mildred Newman and Bernard Berkowitz, with Jean Owen

Ask and It Is Given: Learning to Manifest Your Desires, by Ester and Jerry Hicks

Getting into the Vortex: Guided Meditations CD and User Guide, by Ester and Jerry Hicks

Websites

The Emotional Freedom Technique, Gary Craig

https://www.emofree.com

Create the Life You Love One "Yes" at a Time, Psychotherapist and EFT Master, Carol Look

https://www.carollook.com

For additional Tips, Resources, and Tapping Videos, visit the author's website

http://www.simplythebestresults.com/products/freebies

YouTube Videos

EFT Introduction, Gary Craig

https://www.youtube.com/watch?v=VFKVVP8KXd4

EFT Basic Recipe by Founder Gary Craig

https://www.youtube.com/watch?v=1wG2FA4vfLQ

Quotes Used with Permission

"We can change the story we tell ourselves… and by doing that, we change the future." - Eleanor Brown, author of *The Weird Sisters*. http://www.eleanor-brown.com

"You are the author of your life. You create the story and you can rewrite it." -- Fabienne Fredrickson, http://www.BoldHeart.com

"Journal writing is a voyage to the interior." – Christina Baldwin, http://Peerspirit.com

"When you become conscious of your thoughts, you will gain power over them." – Cheryl C Jones, http://www.SimplytheBestResults.com

"People become attached to their burdens sometimes more than the burdens are attached to them." -- George Bernal Shaw, quote from the *Preface of MISALLIANCE*. Granted permission by, For The Society of Authors.

"Love is what we are born with. Fear is what we learned here." – Marianne Williamson, https://marianne.com/

"Derived from the Greek word "em" (in) and "pathos" (feeling), the term "empath" refers to a person who is able to "feel into" the feelings of others." – Mateo Sol, Awaken Empath: The Ultimate Guide to Emotional, Psychological and Spiritual Healing, https://lonerwolf.com

"Your true power does not come from your physical action, but from your vibrational alignment." -- Abraham (Ester Hicks), https://www.abraham-hicks.com/

"When you have clarity of intention, the Universe conspires with you to make it happen." – Fabienne Fredrickson, http://wwwBoldHeart.com

"What we see depends mainly on what we look for." – John Lubbock

"The quality of your life is determined by the quality of the questions you ask yourself." – Kevin McDonald, https://thecoachingdept.com/

"You can't get to your next best self clinging to who you were yesterday." – Robin Sharma, http://www.RobinSharma.com

About the Author

Cheryl C. Jones is a dynamic facilitator, speaker, and issue eliminator, a.k.a. personal coach. For more than twenty-eight years, she has worked with individuals and small businesses to resolve unsupportive, outdated, and limited thinking so that they can do more, have more, and achieve more.

She is an expert on the topics of interpersonal communication, teamwork, and emotional self-management.

High-profile organizations such as the San Antonio Spurs and Wells Fargo Banks, as well as, very successful small businesses are drawn to work with Cheryl because of her straightforward and down-to-earth demeanor. She offers practical, easy-to-apply techniques to improve communication, efficiency, and camaraderie.

Cheryl is a member of the National Speakers Association and the President of the Austin NSA Chapter. She is an advanced practitioner of the Emotional Freedom Technique (EFT), as well as, several other healing modalities.

Cheryl resides in San Antonio, Texas, with her husband Marvin, their two sons, and their canine companions, Pinot and Comet.